IMPROVING
EMPLOYEE
PERFORMANCE
IN THE
FOODSERVICE
INDUSTRY

FOODSERVICE EMPLOYEE MANAGEMENT SERIES

Staffing Your Foodservice Operation
Retaining Your Foodservice Employees

Improving Employee Performance in the Foodservice Industry

A GUIDE TO
EMPLOYEE DISCIPLINE

KAREN EICH DRUMMOND

VAN NOSTRAND REINHOLD
New York

Library of Congress Catalog Card Number 91-39885
ISBN 0-442-00573-3

Printed in the United States of America.

Van Nostrand Reinhold
115 Fifth Avenue
New York, New York 10003

Chapman and Hall
2-6 Boundary Row
London, SE1 8HN, England

Thomas Nelson Australia
102 Dodds Street
South Melbourne 3205
Victoria, Australia

Nelson Canada
1120 Birchmount Road
Scarborough, Ontario MIK 5G4, Canada

16 15 14 13 12 11 10 9 8 7 6 5 4 3 2 1

Library of Congress Cataloging-in-Publication Data
Drummond, Karen Eich.
    Improving employee performance in the foodservice industry:
a guide to employee discipline / Karen Eich Drummond.
        p. cm.
    Includes bibliographical references (p.   ) and index.
    ISBN 0-442-00573-3
    1. Food service—Personnel management. I. Title.
TX911.3.P4D782   1992
647.95'068'3—dc20   91-39885
                                                     CIP

To current and future foodservice managers:
May your employees be their own source of discipline.

CONTENTS

Preface   ix

1   Introduction to Discipline   1

    Discipline: A Four-Step Process   2
    Approaches to Discipline   4
    Progressive Discipline   6
    Employee Expectations: Due Process   11

2   How to Establish and Communicate Expectations   13

    Developing Performance Standards   14
    Developing a Code of Conduct   14
    Developing Your Discipline or Corrective Action Policy and
        Procedures   19
    Communicating Expectations   33

3   Dealing with Performance Issues   35

    Listening Skills   35
    Reducing Employee Defensiveness   38
    Coaching   38
    Performance Appraisal   43

4   Dealing with Violations of Conduct Rules   61

    Fact-Finding   61
    Disciplinary Interview   62
    Decision Making and Implementation of the Decision   65
    Documentation   65
    Administering Discipline   68

5 Termination 71

Employment-at-Will and Just Cause 72
Termination Policy 75
Alternatives to Dismissal 78
Should This Employee Be Discharged? 81
The Termination Interview 84

6 Special Concerns: Substance Abuse, Attendance
Problems, and Sexual Harassment 91

Substance Abuse 91
Attendance Problems 103
Sexual Harassment 119

7 How to Create a Disciplined Work Force 121

Eight Ways to Create a Disciplined Work Force 122
Sound Selection Procedures 123
Trained Supervisors 134
Emphasis on Mutual Respect and Communication 135

Appendix

Communicating Effectively 137

Bibliography 151

Index 155

Preface

There are very few books written about discipline. Little wonder, it's a topic most of us would prefer to avoid! When most of us think of discipline, we think of punishment, of punishing employees who violate rules or regulations in hopes that they will conform to our standards. The truth is that the word *discipline* is derived from the word *disciple*, which means follower or pupil. *Discipline is not punishment; it means helping your employees become the best possible workers they can.* Punishment should not be the intent of disciplinary action. Rather, discipline should have as its goal the improvement of the employee's future behavior. To apply discipline in any other way can only invite problems such as wrongful discharge suits. The methods that we use to discipline, therefore, include not only reminders or warnings, but also coaching and performance appraisals.

The purpose of this book is to help you use discipline to improve employee performance, not as a way to terminate your employees. Topics to be discussed include positive and negative discipline; how to establish and communicate expectations to your employees; how to deal with performance issues and violations of conduct rules; termination; how to develop substance abuse, sexual harrassment, and attendance policies and deal with these concerns; and how to develop a disciplined work force.

Discipline can be a positive and constructive process rather than negative and confrontational. Read on and you will see how.

IMPROVING
EMPLOYEE
PERFORMANCE
IN THE
FOODSERVICE
INDUSTRY

1

Introduction to Discipline

How do you define discipline?

1. Punishment intended to correct
2. A state of order based on submission to rules and authority
3. Orderly behavior in a place of work
4. Training that reinforces desirable conduct, corrects undesirable conduct, and develops self-discipline

When most of us think of discipline in the workplace, we think of punishment of employees who violate rules or regulations in hopes that they will conform to our standards. The truth is that the word "discipline" is derived from the word "disciple," which means follower or pupil. *Discipline is not punishment; it means helping your employees to become the best possible workers they can be.* Punishment should not be the intent of disciplinary action. Rather, discipline should have as its goal the improvement of the employee's future behavior. To apply discipline in any other way can only invite problems, such as wrongful discharge suits. The methods that we use to discipline, therefore, include not only reminders and warnings, but also coaching and performance appraisals.

Most of your employees want to do a good job and want to conduct themselves in an acceptable manner. When you treat discipline as a way to work with employees so they will meet expectations, you derive numerous benefits.

- Good job performance
- Increased job satisfaction
- Increased employee morale
- Improved productivity
- Consistently high quality of food and service

1

- Improved communication
- Less absenteeism
- Fewer accidents
- Less waste and breakage

This chapter discusses the process of discipline, two different approaches to discipline, the nature of progressive discipline, and employees' expectations of a discipline system.

Discipline: A Four-Step Process

As depicted in Figure 1-1, there are four steps in the discipline process. First, you have to establish your expectations of your employees. This includes writing performance standards, a code of conduct, and a discipline or corrective action policy and procedures. Employees both want and need to know exactly what is expected of them.

Performance standards are observable and measurable criteria by which you can decide whether a job duty is being done correctly. For example, requiring a server to greet guests with a smile and within 2 minutes of their being seated is a performance standard. Standards also help employees know whether or not they are doing their jobs correctly.

A code of conduct states how you expect employees to conduct themselves on the job. For instance, you may address the way employees are to interact with each other and with guests, how employees are to be dressed, the importance of being on time at work, and behaviors that are prohibited. This section outlining prohibited behaviors is usually derived from your discipline or corrective action policy and procedures.

When you have written down what you expect from your employees, the next step is to communicate your expectations to current employees and new hires. Employees can hardly be expected to follow rules they know nothing or little about. Communication of this information starts during the selection process, even before employees are hired. The better informed an applicant is, the more likely he or she will be able to meet standards and follow rules. Once a new employee comes on board, these standards and rules become an important part of orientation and training.

In the third step, you assess or evaluate employees' performance and actions by coaching and conducting performance appraisals. Although some managers think they should evaluate an employee's performance only once a year at peformance appraisal time or when an incident (such as excessive lateness) is brought to their attention,

Fig. 1-1   THE DISCIPLINE PROCESS

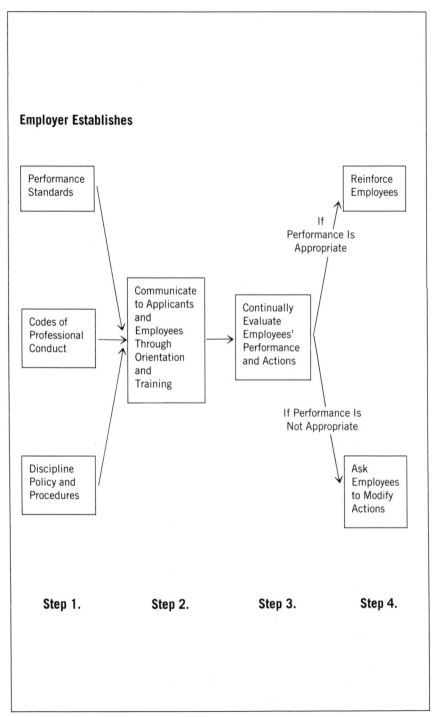

Employer Establishes

Performance Standards

Codes of Professional Conduct

Discipline Policy and Procedures

Communicate to Applicants and Employees Through Orientation and Training

Continually Evaluate Employees' Performance and Actions

If Performance Is Appropriate

Reinforce Employees

If Performance Is Not Appropriate

Ask Employees to Modify Actions

Step 1.   **Step 2.**   **Step 3.**   **Step 4.**

there are many benefits to assessing employee's actions on an ongoing basis.

In the final step, after assessing employee performance and conduct, employees are either praised—their good performance reinforced—or asked to modify their actions. Each of these steps is discussed in detail in this book.

Approaches to Discipline

In the *traditional approach to discipline,* employees are treated like children and are not encouraged to take responsibility for their actions. Instead, they are encouraged to comply with rules, but only to avoid getting into trouble. Each time an employee does something wrong, he or she is warned, chastised, and possibly punished through the loss of pay in the hope that he or she will now conform. This person is thought of as a problem employee instead of one who deserves respect and support to correct a problem situation.

When a supervisor sits down with an employee to discuss an incident, the employee is blamed for some personal shortcoming and receives no positive feedback. Little is said about what could be done in the future to correct the concern, except for a threat of punishment should such an incident happen again. The supervisor does not invite the employee to speak, and when the employee tries to speak in self-defense, the supervisor takes an adversarial, instead of a helpful, position. The supervisor is very uncomfortable during the entire meeting and may even tell the employee, "My boss made me do this."

All in all, the meeting is intimidating and destructive to the employee's self-respect. The employee is left to bring about a change without any support or guidance. No one will help, but you can bet everyone will be watching. If the employee manages to correct the problem, the only reward is not getting into trouble again. For the supervisor, the meeting is no picnic either. Without question, discipline is one of supervisors' most disliked and difficult tasks, partly because they are forced to buy into an established system they did not shape. Some live with their employees' poor behavior until the situation becomes impossible, because they feel uncomfortable in reprimanding an employee and laying down the law.

Punishment is the hallmark of the traditional approach. In most discipline systems, written warnings and suspension without pay are common punitive features. Unfortunately, punishment tends to

Produce short-term changes in behavior
Do little to point out or encourage desirable behaviors

Create anger and resentment, which may lead to hostility and retaliation

Decrease an employee's sense of commitment to his or her job, which may result in "get by" performance

Does an employee who returns from a three-day suspension without pay usually feel good about the employer and endeavor to do a great job? Actually, employees frequently feel that once they have endured their punishment, they have paid their debt and are absolved of wrongdoing. They may feel that nothing more needs to be done, when just the opposite is true. The outcome is that nothing has been done to deal effectively with the problem and its cause.

Using another approach, *positive discipline,* we no longer look at discipline as something that a supervisor *does to* an employee. Rather, employees themselves must be the real source of discipline. This approach is based on building employee commitment to the goals and expectations of the company, not ripping it apart as so often happens in traditional systems. Instead of telling your employees, "I will discipline you," you continually let them know, "I expect you to be disciplined." Instead of just catching people when they do something wrong and saying, "You must comply or else," you work on catching employees doing something right and praise their actions. This discipline system is used to keep employees, not get rid of them. Instead of being confined to warning, suspending, and firing employees, discipline becomes a part of hiring, orientation, training, coaching, and supervision.

Following are more features of a positive approach.

- The treatment of the employee as an adult
- A focus on defining the problem behavior and finding its solution
- A supervisory role of helping and supporting the employee
- Mutual decision making
- A focus on the future
- An emphasis on the impact of inappropriate behavior on the success of the operation
- Positive reinforcement of employees who have shown improvement

Another major distinction of the positive approach is that punishment is removed. There continues to be correction, but oral and written reminders replace warnings, and a "decision day" replaces a suspension. The purpose of a reminder is to remind the employee of the employer's expectations and the employee's responsibility for meeting them. The supervisor functions as a coach instead of a judge and supports the employee in solving the problem for the future.

A decision day is a day off with pay, during which the employee is asked to consider his or her future by deciding whether to commit to the required change. When the employee returns to work, he or she advises the supervisor of his or her decision—either to work on improving, or to resign and find employment elsewhere. By paying the employee to take this decision day, a supervisor can avoid the anger and resentment with which an employee may otherwise return to the job. This paid suspension is evidence that the company wants the employee to take responsibility for appropriate behavior and make the changes needed for continued employment. Although managers frequently wonder whether employees will abuse the decision day approach, their concern has proved to be unfounded. Most employees take it quite seriously.

In organizations using a positive discipline system, important benefits have been evident. There were fewer disciplinary discussions and terminations, problem situations were addressed and resolved faster, and managers reported fewer immature and emotional behaviors when confronting employees as mature adults. Because managers were no longer required to be punitive and judgmental, they tended to deal with problems more quickly. In general, unions were supportive of the idea of employees' being responsible for their own actions. Employees also liked being treated as adults and being recognized for good performance. Last, but perhaps most important, because the emphasis is on building commitment rather than compliance to rules, employees have exhibited greater commitment to high performance and achieving the goals of the organization.

Table 1-1 summarizes the differences between the traditional and the positive approaches.

Progressive Discipline

Progressive discipline applies corrective measures, such as verbal and written warnings, in increasing degrees or steps. A typical progression for a traditional system consists of a verbal warning, written warning (there may be more than one), suspension (usually from 1 to 10 days), and termination (Fig. 1-2). Each step in the process contains an added factor meant to impress on the employee a greater urgency to comply. An employee, therefore, is rarely terminated for a first offense, unless it is for an act of gross misconduct such as theft. The goal of the progressive discipline system is to give the employee an opportunity

Table 1-1 Approaches to Discipline

	Traditional	*Positive*
Goal	Build compliance	Build commitment
Purpose	Use punishment and threats of further negative action to get employee to comply	Remind employee of his or her responsibility to meet performance and conduct standards
Emphasis	Catching employees who break rules and punishing them	Positively reinforcing employees when they do a good job and, when an employee is having a problem, gaining the employee's agreement to improve
Time focus	Past	Future
Responsibility for action	Supervisor	Employee
Employee treated as	Child	Adult
Supervisor's role	Judge and jury	Coach
Steps involved	Verbal warning Written warning Suspension without pay Termination	Verbal reminder Written reminder Decision day with pay Resignation or termination

to bring his or her conduct into compliance with workplace standards and rules.

Following is an example of how progressive discipline works in a traditional system.

1. An employee violates the attendance policy and is given a verbal warning. He is told that if this happens again during the next 3 months, the next step will be a written warning. This is noted in a supervisor's log, in an employee incident file, or in a memo.

Fig. 1-2 PROGRESSIVE DISCIPLINE IN THE TRADITIONAL APPROACH

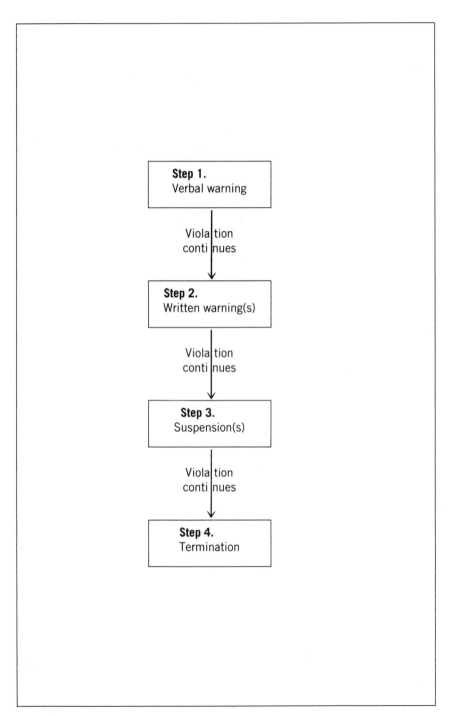

2. The employee's attendance problem does not improve, and the employee receives a written warning 2 months later. It states that if he has the same, or a similar, problem during the next 3 months, he will be suspended for 3 days without pay. The written warning is put into his personnel file.
3. The employee's attendance problem becomes worse and he is given, along with the 3 days' suspension without pay, a final warning that if things do not improve during the next 3 months, he will be fired.
4. Unfortunately the employee violates the attendance policy within 3 months, and he is terminated.

It is in the best interest of both the employer and the employee to use the progressive discipline system in the case of conduct rule violations. Since many problems are resolved through early steps, such as verbal warnings, the employer can often correct situations quickly and efficiently. For employees, the progressive discipline system provides the security that they will not lose their jobs without notice, unless their actions are cause for immediate dismissal.

In a positive discipline system, the first step is a counseling session between the employee and the manager in which the manager works on gaining the employee's agreement to solve the problem. The good business reasons underlying the rule or standard are explained. The manager does not reprimand the employee nor threaten further disciplinary action. Instead, the emphasis is on confronting the employee, in a mature and supportive manner, with the need to change. The employee is reminded that it is his or her responsibility for appropriate performance and behavior. A note of this meeting is put into the manager's file. Upon follow-up, if the problem has not been resolved, there is a second counseling session in which the manager mentions again that improvement is the employee's responsibility, and the manager helps to work on a solution. A written solution is drawn up and a copy is given to the employee (Fig. 1-3).

If, after the second conference, the problem is still not resolved or at least improved, the employee is allowed a decision-making leave of 1 or more days with pay. The purpose of paying for the leave is to prevent any hostility and to show the individual that the organization wants to help him or her. The employee is given the time off to decide whether he or she is willing to meet the standards. Upon return from the leave, the employee is asked to advise the supervisor of the decision: either to try to meet the standards or to resign. If the employee stays, but problems continue, termination is the next step. Because positive discipline has a "just cause" focus, terminations will stand up in court.

Fig. 1-3 DOCUMENTATION OF POSITIVE DISCIPLINE STEP

MEMO

TO: John Johnson, Dishwasher
FROM: Ray Jones, Kitchen Manager
DATE: January 5, 1992
SUBJECT: Second Conference on Attendance Problem, 1/5/92

Statement of Problem: At the end of the previous quarter, John had
excessive absenteeism, having missed 6 days of work because of sickness
during that period of time. He was counseled on October 2, 1991 about the
problem as per memo of October 3, 1991. During this quarter (October 1
to December 31, 1991) John was again absent from his job for 6 days
because of sickness: October 31, November 14–16, December 26,
December 31.

Employee's Explanation: Most of John's sick days are caused by the illness
of his wife and child.

Solution: John says he will try to locate someone to look after his wife and
child when they are sick. I suggested any available relatives or friends. I
will follow up with John on February 15, 1992.

      Supervisor's Signature   Date

Employee Agreement:

   I agree with the solution and will start making arrangements so this
problem does not occur again. I understand that if I am sick more than 3
days in this quarter, I will be given a decision-making leave.

      Supervisor's Signature   Date

Employee Expectations: Due Process

Essential to having disciplined employees is the realization that employees have a right to a fair and appropriate discipline system. Following are the key components of a discipline system that meets the realistic expectations of employees as well as many legal requirements.

Employees have the right to know what is expected of them and what will happen when they do not fulfill those expectations. There must be explicit oral or written communication to employees informing them of rules and penalties. Where it can be proven that an employee lacked knowledge about certain rules, discipline is rarely found to be appropriate.

The employee has a right to consistent and predictable responses by the employer when there are performance problems or rule violations. Consistency means treating similar situations in a similar way. Predictability means reacting in the same way each time a certain situation occurs, and increases the chances that employees will comply because they know their behavior—either poor or good—will not be ignored.

The employee has a right to unbiased discipline based on accurate facts. An effective discipline system is based on a supervisor's gathering facts with an open mind before a judgment is made. It is easy to jump to conclusions when, for instance, you hear that the dish room was left a mess last night and you feel sure that the culprit was that part-time dishwasher again. Numerous discharge and discipline cases have been reversed or revised because a manager's judgment was based on wrongful assumptions, hearsay, or unjustified jumps in logic. It is not required that the evidence be beyond a reasonable doubt or conclusive, but it must be substantial. In addition to keeping an open mind, fact-finding requires maintaining good records or documentation.

The employee has a right to know the facts, acknowledge or question them, and present a defense before a disciplinary decision is made. After fact-finding is completed, sit down with the employee and present him or her with the alleged charges and the facts substantiating them. Next, give the employee a chance to defend him- or herself in a setting where he or she does not feel threatened, railroaded, or oppressed. In other words, give the employee his or her "day in court." Just as the employee can make a mistake, so can you. Unfortunately, the typical meeting between a manager and an employee in the manager's office is often threatening to the employee who, even when given the chance to present a defense, may feel too intimidated to do so. Usually this situation is helped by having the employee bring another person, such as a peer, into the disciplinary meeting.

The employee has the right to appeal the disciplinary decision. Whenever disciplinary action is taken, the employee involved should be reminded to use the established appeal procedure if he or she feels the action was unfair.

The employee has the right to progressive discipline.

The employee has a right to be considered as an individual. When deterrmining whether an employee is to be disciplined, and to what extent, you need to consider the employee's prior performance and discipline record. The need to be consistent in applying discipline does not restrain you from considering an employee's record when determining the punishment. In other words, given the same violation by two different employees, you can give the employee with the better record a lighter punishment without its constituting true discrimination. There is some room for the exercise of judgment and for individual treatment.

2

How to Establish and Communicate Expectations

As a supervisor, you have the right to expect employees to act in certain ways, such as being on time, putting in a full day's work, responding positively to supervision, getting along with fellow employees, and complying with rules and regulations. Starting with the staffing process and continuing during orientation, you must clearly lay out what you expect of your applicants and new hires, including how well they perform job duties and how they conduct themselves. If you do not, you risk having disgruntled employees who often resign during the first month or whom you terminate during probation because "they just did not seem to be working out."

This chapter explains how to develop performance standards and a code of conduct, two major tools to ensure employee understanding of your expectations. There is also a thorough discussion on developing a discipline or corrective action policy and procedures.

First, let us consider what constitutes unacceptable behavior. Most unacceptable behavior falls into one of two categories.

- Misconduct that is due to a conscious, and often willful, decision by the employee, such as stealing
- Performance problems that are often beyond the employee's control, perhaps as a result of inadequate training, improper tools, or personal inabilities

Your discipline or corrective action policy and procedures should address the first category of behavior; they should be truly disciplinary in nature. You can work on the second category of behavior with the employee through coaching and performance appraisals, which are thoroughly discussed in the next chapter.

Developing Performance Standards

Performance standards translate job duties into levels of acceptable or unacceptable performance. For example, a performance standard for servers might read: "Greets customers within 3 minutes of being seated." Performance standards should be job-based, observable, measurable, and realistic.

Performance standards may involve quantities, such as the number of covers or tables a server can tend to, or qualities, such as an employee's ability to be helpful. Standards may also discuss speed or accuracy. Vague words such as "approximately," "appropriate," "reasonable," and "adequate" should be avoided. Figure 2-1 lists performance standards for a cook.

Developing a Code of Conduct

A code of conduct (Fig. 2-2) should discuss clearly the types of behaviors you expect, and those you do not expect, from your employees. This is the primary tool for communicating the do's and don'ts of your workplace to your employees. Following are areas of employee conduct you may want to include.

- Compliance with company policies and procedures
- Compliance with sanitation and safety rules
- Compliance with attendance rules
- Meeting job performance standards
- Cooperative and effective relationships with co-workers, guests, and supervisors
- Protection of company property
- Honesty in company-related matters
- Substance abuse

The code of conduct also summarizes your discipline or corrective action policy and procedures, to be discussed next, including unsatisfactory behaviors and their consequences. This can be done in a variety of ways. At one extreme, you may simply make a broad statement of responsibility such as the following:

When employees do not meet our code of conduct, the company, at its discretion, will take appropriate corrective action. Based on the nature of the offense and the employee's record, corrective action may include a verbal warning, written warning, probation,

Fig. 2-1   PERFORMANCE STANDARDS FOR HEAD COOK

PERFORMANCE STANDARDS—HEAD COOK

Major Duties and Responsibilities	Evaluation Criteria Performance meets the standard when performed 90% of the time:
1. Prepares kitchen for day's activities.	1a. Daily picks up and signs for the keys from the switchboard. Unlocks refrigerators, turns on steam tables, toaster, heating elements for plates and bottoms, turns on circuit breakers in storeroom for ovens, grill, mixers, tilt fryer, and deep fat fryer.
2. Ensures that food supplies are adequate for the day's menus.	2a. Checks menus for items to be pulled from freezer and thawed in refrigerator.
	2b. Checks that proper amounts of food are available to prepare meals at all times.
	2c. Limits leftovers and uses all leftover items possible in other dishes, safely, while maintaining their tastiness.
3. Ensures that meals are served on time and are of highest quality.	3a. Checks with cooks and management to make sure that all meals will be ready on time.
	3b. Inspects food to make sure that it meets quality standards (consistency, texture, seasoning, and temperature).
	3c. Follows standardized recipes.
	3d. Follows through on special instructions left by the Food and Beverage Director or the assistant.
	3e. Meals are attractively garnished.
4. Oversees preparation of all hot food.	4a. Follows production sheets.

Fig. 2-1   Continued

Major Duties and Responsibilities	Evaluation Criteria Performance meets the standard when performed 90% of the time:
5. Assists in planning for advance preparation, cafeteria weekly menu, and special functions.	5a. Provides useful input into planning activities.
6. Ensures cleanliness and neatness of cooks' area.	6a. Cook's area passes weekly sanitation inspection.
7. Maintains equipment in good working order.	7a. Checks equipment to ensure that it works properly and reports problems to Food and Beverage Director.
8. Instructs cooks and cooks' helpers.	8a. Fully instructs cooks on meals and advance preparation. 8b. Conducts cooks' meetings on weekly basis.
9. Maintains refrigerators and storage areas.	9a. Checks that all foods are properly stocked, labeled, and dated in refrigerators and other storage areas designated for food items on a daily basis. 9b. Uses food items on first-in, first-out basis to minimize waste. 9c. Uses leftovers within 24 hours to assure safe food handling practice.

Fig. 2-2 SAMPLE GUIDELINES FOR EMPLOYEE COOPERATION AND DISCIPLINE (CODE OF CONDUCT)

Common sense, good judgment, and appropriate behavior are part of the essential responsibilities of every employee. The following information is intended to provide you with the actual guidelines for cooperation during the regular performance of your work—in essence, the rules and regulations.

Level I Infractions

A progressive four-step disciplinary process will be followed in cases involving the infractions listed below, which include a written warning for the first offense, a second written warning for the second offense, a probation period of 90 days for the third offense, and termination for the fourth offense when it occurs during the probationary period. If you successfully complete the probationary period and the infraction occurs, you will be placed back on probation for another 90 days. An employee may be placed on probation only two times during a sliding 24-month period from the date of the infraction that led to the initiation of the first probation.

Documentation of disciplinary action pertaining to infractions will be removed from your personnel record once it becomes 24 months old.

—Unauthorized and/or unscheduled absence from duty or work location.
—Unauthorized and/or unscheduled lateness for duty.
—Failure to comply with departmental notification requirements in cases of unauthorized absences, illness, and/or lateness.
—Failure to comply with company photo-identification or related security policies.
—Presence in unauthorized areas.
—Failure to perform duties as assigned or to a reasonably satisfactory degree.
—Conducting raffles, pools, or other games of chance on premises without approval.
—Selling or advertising merchandise, tickets, or services without prior written approval by management.
—Creating an unsafe or unsanitary condition or contributing to such conditions.
—Smoking in unauthorized areas.
—Unauthorized parking of vehicles on company property.
—Unauthorized use of company mails, telephones, equipment, or supplies in personal business.
—Excessive unscheduled absences (unscheduled time lost from work regardless of reason, including sick time and emergency personal days).
—Excessive failure to punch in or out or to use authorized time and attendance reader.

Fig. 2-2 Continued

—Disregard of appearance, uniforms, dress, or personal hygiene that is detrimental to departmental standards.

—Distribution of unauthorized literature/pamphlets by employees during working time* or in working and guest areas.

—Solicitation for unauthorized purposes during working time* or in working and guest areas.

* Working time does not include meal breaks, work breaks or any time an employee is not working.

Gross Infractions—Level II

In cases involving the gross infractions listed below, a three-step process will be followed, which involves a suspension without pay, investigation of the charges, and a disciplinary review meeting.

You are permitted to have other company persons or employees attend the meeting to provide support or factual information pertaining to the charges. As a result of the meeting, one of the following three actions will occur:

1. Reinstatement with full back pay.
2. Reinstatement with the suspension upheld (without pay).
3. Termination.

Level II Infractions

—Falsification of any company document or record.

—Sleeping while on duty.

—Direct or tacit refusal to comply with a supervisor's instructions or to perform a job assignment.

—Failure to properly render service to a guest when such service is within the regular and/or reasonable scope of an employee's duties, or is required in a bona fide emergency.

—Use of abusive language and unnecessary shouting in a guest area or general work area.

—Reporting for duty in a condition unfit for proper performance of assigned work.

—Use or unauthorized possession of intoxicants, drugs or similar substances on company premises without written or administrative approval.

—Use or possession of a weapon on company premises.

—Misappropriation, unauthorized possession, or misuse of property belonging to the company, or any employee, or guest.

Fig. 2-2   Continued

—Unauthorized possession, misuse, reading, or copying of company
documents or records, or disclosure of information of such records to
unauthorized persons.
—Threatening, intimidating, or coercing of another employee or guest,
including verbal or physical altercations or related disorderly conduct.
—Any illegal act or conduct on company premises.
—Any act or conduct that is seriously detrimental to company operations.

Source: Adapted from *You and Jersey Shore Medical Center* (an employee
handbook), Neptune, NJ. Reprinted with permission.

suspension, or discharge. Gross misconduct will result in immediate discharge.

One advantage of this approach is that it omits any listing of unacceptable behaviors and is therefore more positive in tone. This type of positive approach probably works better with exempt or managerial employees than hourly, often entry-level, foodservice employees.

At the other extreme is a code that details at great length specific punishments for each unsatisfactory type of behavior (Fig. 2-3). The use of this kind of table tends to encourage a cookbook approach to discipline, which fails to take into account the unique circumstances of each situation. A middle road that does not lock the supervisor into rigid rules, but gives the employee sufficient notice, will be discussed next.

Developing Your Discipline or Corrective Action Policy and Procedures

Discipline or corrective action policy and procedures usually cover the following topics.

- Discipline or corrective action guidelines
- Employee grievance policy and procedures
- Termination policy and procedures (covered in Chapter 5)

Figure 2-4 lists questions that will guide you in the development of your policy and procedures. Figure 2-5 is a sample policy and procedures statement.

Fig. 2-3 DETAILED CODE OF CONDUCT

Offense	Verbal Warning	Written Warning	Suspension	Dismissal
Excessive tardiness or absenteeism	First step	Second step	Third step	Fourth step
Absent from work area	First step	Second step	Third step	Fourth step
Failure to perform job duties satisfactorily	First step	Second step	Third step	Fourth step
Creating an unsafe or unsanitary condition		First step	Second step	Third step
Absent for one day without calling in		First step	Second step	Third step
Abuse of breaktime		First step	Second step	Third step
Unfit for duty			First step	Second step
Using abusive language			First step	Second step
Sleeping on duty			First step	Second step
Insubordination			First step	Second step
Fighting			First step	Second step
Falsification of company documents				Immediate dismissal
Theft				Immediate dismissal
Possession or use of alcohol or non-prescribed drugs during working time or on company property				Immediate dismissal

**Fig. 2-4   QUESTIONS TO CONSIDER WHEN DEVELOPING
A DISCIPLINE POLICY AND PROCEDURE**

Discipline System

1. Which will be acceptable—a traditional or a positive discipline system? Or will a system based on selected characteristics of both systems be acceptable?
2. Should employees be reminded, or warned?
3. Should employees be suspended without pay, or given paid decision days?

Discipline or Corrective Action Guidelines

4. Should discipline or corrective action guidelines be broad and undefined, or detailed? If detailed, how specific should they be?
5. Will acts of gross misconduct be identified, along with their consequences?
6. Will guidelines for handling misconduct be kept separate from those addressing performance problems?
7. Concerning attendance problems, will you use an excuse-based or a no-fault system?

Grievance Procedure

8. Which will be acceptable—an informal or a formal system? Will both be acceptable?

Fig. 2-5 SAMPLE DISCIPLINE POLICIES AND PROCEDURES STATEMENT

PERSONNEL POLICIES AND PROCEDURES

DISTRIBUTION:	Managerial/ Supervisory Staff	SUBJECT:	Guidelines for Cooperation and Discipline

EFFECTIVE DATE   1/1/82   FILE UNDER SECTION   IX   NO.   9.2

REVISION DATE.   1/1/90   APPROVED BY:

ALL REVISIONS ARE MARKED BY AN ASTERISK (*)

Policy Statement

This Policy and Procedures change is designed to assist all members of the staff involved in the administration of a progressive disciplinary process. It is also intended to improve the communication to all employees of the actual Guidelines for Cooperation in the regular performance of their work—in essence, the rules and regulations.

Procedures

There will be formally defined rules and regulations for all employees, known as Guidelines for Cooperation, which will be communicated to all employees on staff and new employees at the time of hiring.

These guidelines will be centrally administrated and uniformly interpreted to ensure equity of application in the departments.

Employees who exhibit problem behavior, i.e., behavior that, if unchecked, can lead to serious problems or over the long term can contribute to performance problems, should be approached by the supervisor and the situation discussed with the employee. It is the supervisor's discretion to discuss the situation with the employee or to begin the disciplinary process.

* A progressive four-step disciplinary process will be followed in cases involving Level I infractions. In cases involving Level II (gross) infractions, where discharges from staff are requested, a three-step process will be followed which involves a three-day suspension without pay, investigation of charges, and a Disciplinary Review Process Meeting to establish upholding the suspension termination, or reinstatement. In cases that result in a suspension or termination, the employee may request a Board of Review through their general manager.

When an employee is arrested in connection with an external matter, the employee is placed on suspension without pay pending the outcome of the civil hearing. If the employee is vindicated, employee status can be reinstated without back pay. If convicted, the employee will be terminated.

The following procedures are not intended to cover every situation that arises. Because each disciplinary situation is different, this procedure may not always be exactly followed.

Fig. 2-5   Continued

Procedure for Level I Infractions

1. Whenever an employee violates one or more infractions in the same level and the supervisor determines that the disciplinary process should be initiated (refer to the third paragraph under Policy Statement), an Employee Disciplinary Notice is prepared. The "First Warning" block is checked. The specific infraction(s) involved and all pertinent data, i.e., date, time, places, etc., are included. The four-part form is distributed according to the instructions on the form.

2. The Employee Disciplinary Notice is to be issued within a reasonable time (5 working days) after the infraction(s) occurs and in as confidential a setting as possible. The employee has a right to write a rebuttal and/or refuse to sign the notice. A witness should be called in cases when an employee refuses to sign the notice—to witness only the refusal to sign, not the details of the notice's contents. The witness preferably should be at the supervisory level.

*3. A second violation of one or more infractions in the same level that occurs within 12 months from the initiation of the first warning, is to be documented on an Employee Disciplinary Notice form as a second warning.

*4. A third violation of one or more infractions in the same level that occurs within 12 months from the initiation of the second warning, is to be documented on an Employee Disciplinary Notice form as a final warning, and the employee will be placed on probation.

*5. A next violation of one or more infractions in the same level that occurs within 12 months from the initiation of the third (final) warning, is to be documented on an Employee Disciplinary Notice form and will serve as a termination notice to the employee.

Examples of Level I Infractions

—Unauthorized and/or unscheduled absence from duty or work location
—Unauthorized and/or unscheduled lateness for duty
—Failure to comply with departmental notification requirements in cases of unauthorized absences, illness, and/or lateness
—Failure to comply with company photo-identification or related security policies
—Presence in unauthorized areas
—Failure to perform duties as assigned or to a reasonably satisfactory degree
—Conducting raffles, pools, or other games of chance on premises without approval
—Selling or advertising merchandise, tickets, or services without prior written approval by management
—Creating an unsafe or unsanitary condition or contributing to such conditions
—Smoking in unauthorized areas
—Unauthorized parking of vehicles on company property
—Unauthorized use of company mails, telephones, equipment, or supplies in personal business
—Excessive unscheduled absences (unscheduled time lost from work regardless of reason, including sick time and emergency personal days)
—Excessive failure to punch in or out or to use authorized time and attendance reader

Fig. 2-5   Continued

—Disregard of appearance, uniforms, dress, or personal hygiene that is detrimental to departmental standards

—Distribuion of unauthorized literature/pamphlets by employees during working time* or in working and guest areas

—Solicitation for unauthorized purposes during working time* or in working and guest areas

* Working time does not include meal breaks, work breaks, or any time an employee is not working.

Procedure for Level II (Gross Infractions)

1. The Employee Disciplinary Notice and suspension are to be issued within a reasonable time after the infraction(s) occurs and in as confidential a setting as possible. The employee has the right to write a rebuttal and/or to refuse to sign the notice. A witness should be called in cases when the employee refuses to sign the notice—to witness only the refusal to sign, not the details of the notice's contents. The witness preferably should be at the supervisory level.

2. No employee will be discharged from staff without the Disciplinary Review Process. The employee shall be placed on suspension without pay pending investigation and the Disciplinary Review Process meeting.

*3. The matter will be investigated and the Disciplinary Review meeting will then be scheduled within 2 working days of the date the suspension began.

4. The persons present at the Disciplinary Review meeting may include the employee(s), supervisor of the employee and/or the department manager, the general manager and the director of personnel management as the Disciplinary Review officer.

5. The employee will be permitted to have other approved employees or other persons present at the Disciplinary Review Process meeting to give factual data. A written request from the employee to the director of personnel management must be received for review and approval at least 1 working day in advance of the meeting. The director of personnel management is authorized to reject the presence of any persons at the meeting who have not been previously approved to appear. All information presented at the meeting must be true and factual. Failure in this respect will eliminate consideration of the information presented.

6. Employee Disciplinary Notice forms, Employee Performance Appraisals, Letters of Commendation, and all related aspects of an employee's personnel profile may be considered in the deliberations of the Disciplinary Review officer, inclusive from the original date of hire. All pertinent factual data and/or testimony will be considered during the Disciplinary Review Process, and a final decision rendered within 5 working days after the meeting.

Examples of Level II (Gross) Infractions

The following are classified as gross infractions and will result in suspension without pay pending investigation and a Disciplinary Review Process meeting to establish upholding the suspension, termination, or reinstatement:

Fig. 2-5 Continued

—Falsification of any company document or record.
—Sleeping while on duty.
—Direct or tacit refusal to comply with a supervisor's instructions or perform a job assignment.
—Failure to properly render service to a guest, when such service is within the regular and/or reasonable scope of an employee's duties, or is required in a bona fide emergency.
—Use of abusive language and unnecessary shouting in a public contact or general work area.
—Reporting for duty in a condition which is unfit for proper performance of assigned work.
—Use, or unauthorized possession of intoxicants, drugs, or similar substances, on premises without written medical or Administrative approval.
—Use, or possession of a weapon on premises.
—Misappropriation, unauthorized possession or misuse of property belonging to the company or any employees or guest.
—Unauthorized possession, misuse, reading or copying of company documents or records, of disclosure of information of such records to unauthorized persons.
—Threatening, intimidating, or coercing of another employee or guest, including verbal or physical altercations or related disorderly conduct.
—Any illegal act or conduct on company property.
—Any act or conduct which is seriously detrimental to company operations.

Any questions regarding this Policy and Procedure may be directed to the Director of Personnel Management.

FLOW CHART

DISCIPLINE

Level I Infractions	Level II Infractions (Gross)
STEP 1 Warning	STEP 1 Suspended by supervisor (without pay)
↓	↓
STEP 2 Warning	STEP 2 Investigation of the offense
↓	↓
STEP 3 Probation	STEP 3 Disciplinary Review Process meeting to establish:
STEP 4 Termination when infraction occurs during probation.	1. Upholding suspension (3 days).
	2. Termination.
	3. Reinstatement.
↓	↓
An employee terminated may request a Board of Review through the general manager.	An employee terminated may request a Board of Review through the general manager.

Source: Adapted from Personnel Policies and Procedures, Jersey Shore Medical Center, Neptune, NJ. Reprinted with permission.

25

DISCIPLINE OR CORRECTIVE ACTION GUIDELINES

Your discipline or corrective action guidelines should be just that, guidelines to direct you when an employee's actions have been inappropriate. They should be specific enough to give you adequate direction but not so inflexible that you must handle every disciplinary situation in exactly the same way. Every employee is different; every disciplinary situation is different. There are different circumstances and consequences. Consistency is important, but so is flexibility. For example, it would be unfair to treat these two people the same: a long-term satisfactory employee who falls asleep during a break one day after taking care of her sick spouse the previous night; and another employee on probation who falls asleep at the wheel while delivering pizzas, after bragging about partying until 3 o'clock that morning. Although both situations involve sleeping on the job, the circumstances surrounding each situation, and the consequences, are vastly different. As long as you apply the same set of goals and values to each situation, you can treat each case individually *and* consistently.

The first step in the process of developing discipline guidelines is to *identify inappropriate behaviors that may require corrective action.* Some operators categorize discipline problems into minor and major infractions. Minor infractions do little harm to the operation but can be serious if they occur frequently or together with another infraction. Examples include the following:

Excessive absenteeism and/or tardiness
Leaving the work area without supervisor's permission
Abuse of break times and meal periods
Smoking in a nonsmoking area
Improper use of company telephones

Major infractions are more serious and comprise dishonest, illegal, and other such acts. Examples include the following:

Sleeping while on duty
Refusal to carry out reasonable assignments from an authorized superior
Fighting on company property
Discourteous treatment of guests or co-workers, including harassing, coercing, threatening, or intimidating others
Violation or neglect of safety rules or contributing to hazardous conditions

Knowingly falsifying employment records such as time-worked records

Knowingly falsifying guest checks or other work records

Gambling on premises

Unauthorized destruction or theft of company property

Possession, display, or use of firearms or other dangerous weapons while on company property

Use or possession of controlled substances while on company property

You may want to list a number of these as grounds for immediate dismissal.

If you do list examples of unacceptable behaviors, be sure to make a statement such as this:

The following policy and procedures are not intended to cover every situation that arises.

When developing your guidelines, *keep in mind the kind of behavior that would be expected from a reasonable person* in a given situation. Is it reasonable to allow an employee to be absent 10 days in a year? It probably is, particularly if your sick-day policy allows 10 days per year.

If you specify punishments in your guidelines, *incorporate reasonable and appropriate punishments.* Punishment should fit the infraction and be reasonably related to the safe and efficient operation of the foodservice. The punishment should be neither so light as to be ignored nor so heavy as to do harm. Also be sure to include a statement such as this:

Because each disciplinary situation is unique, this policy and procedure may not always be exactly followed or used.

If you do not want to specify punishments, you can make a general statement such as this:

Violation of our Code of Conduct may lead to disciplinary action, up to and including immediate dismissal.

Include a time limit, and perhaps other conditions, for the removal of any corrective action documentation from the employees' files. For example, you may specify that any documentation more than 1 year old is to be removed from the file. Employees often see such documentation as a hindrance to advancement or a satisfactory evaluation. In other words, employees may feel they have little reason to excel if corrective action documentation is on file.

Include information on how new employee performance and misconduct problems will be handled. Many employers require a probation period of 90 days for new employees. During the probationary period, employers often state either party may terminate the relationship at any time without notice. Thus, if performance or misconduct problems surface and you have little faith that they can be corrected, you can terminate the employee.

Finally, be sure to *use clear, understandable language.*

EMPLOYEE GRIEVANCE POLICY AND PROCEDURES

A grievance procedure is any system set up for an employee to question, complain, or appeal a supervisor's decision. In a union setting, a grievance procedure is a formal mechanism for processing employee complaints. In a nonunion setting, employers use formal, and sometimes informal, methods to resolve complaints. In this case, the grievance procedure may be called by another name so as to distinguish it from that used in a union setting. Examples of such terms include concerns procedure, problems resolution procedures, or employee communication procedures. Whichever name is used for an employee grievance procedure, its purposes remain the same:

To ensure fair and considerate treatment of employees by giving them a hearing on their complaints, questions, and concerns
To give the company a way to handle complaints quickly and to everyone's satisfaction
To avoid expensive lawsuits by settling problems internally

In a nonunion setting, grievance procedures are also used to reduce the threat of unionization.

In your policy and procedures statement, be sure to include the following:

The goals
The system(s) and procedures for resolving grievances
Protection of employee from retaliation

Systems for resolving grievances fall into two categories: informal and formal. Informal systems include the open-door policy. Formal systems include a step procedure and peer review. Every system should meet the following minimum criteria: easy to use, prompt, and fair.

Many managers claim to have an *open-door policy;* that is, their employees are welcome to enter the office with any complaints, concerns, or questions. The policy may be very loose, inviting employees to discuss any problem with their supervisors or any other managers, including top management, or it may be more structured. For example, the policy may direct employees to the human resource department after speaking, without resolution, to their supervisor.

Unfortunately, open-door policies do not always work as planned, either because managers do not really keep their doors open or because the employees feel the invitation is too vague to assure that their concerns will be taken seriously and resolved fairly. Some employees are just too shy and reluctant to use this option. In many cases the employees have already discussed their concerns with their supervisor without finding satisfaction, and feel that they risk retaliation if they go further. In addition, managers run the risk of rendering arbitrary or inconsistent decisions and making the lower-level supervisors appear ineffective to the employees.

In some circumstances, an open-door policy can work. It probably works better in smaller companies where everyone knows the managers and there has been a tradition of listening in a fair and open-minded manner to employees' complaints.

It is not uncommon for a company to have a grievance procedure that combines an open-door policy with a *step grievance procedure.*

Example of a Step Grievance Procedure

- *First Step.* The employee is asked to discuss the concern with his or her immediate supervisor in hope of resolving the issue. Many grievances can be and are resolved at this step. A grievance is often due to a misunderstanding which, if the supervisor handles the situation appropriately, can be easily settled.
- *Second Step.* If the first step does not produce satisfaction for the employee, he or she is now asked to put the grievance into writing and submit it to the department head. By writing out the grievance, the employee is forced to think through the complaint which, if petty or irrational, may make the employee forget about it. If the grievance is worthwhile, the written submission provides all parties involved with a clear and similar idea as to its nature. There is

now a meeting to resolve the grievance between the employee, immediate supervisor, and department head.

- *Third Step.* If still not satisfied, the employee can submit the grievance notice to the director of human resources, who will review it and conduct a hearing with all parties.
- *Fourth Step.* The final step includes a right to appeal the case to a neutral outside party, such as an arbitrator. Arbitration of grievances by a mutually selected neutral party is common in union settings but rare in nonunion settings. In nonunion settings, the peer review process, to be discussed below, may be used.

There are usually time limits for each step to better ensure a just solution; after all, justice delayed is justice denied. Specify how much time the supervisor, or other individual, has to respond to the employee's grievance, as well as how the grievance is to be documented. The use of a standardized form (Fig. 2-6) is helpful to both the employee and the supervisor.

Step review procedures work best when the problem is resolved at the lowest possible level, where the individuals are the most likely to be familiar with the circumstances and most concerned about its outcome. Unfortunately, as the steps proceed, the first-line supervisor is bypassed and both the supervisor and the employee may become more interested in "winning" than coming to a mutual agreement.

In the case of *peer review*, grievances are submitted to a group including peers, and sometimes managers, who function much like a jury. The employee can usually choose which employees, who are specially trained, will be on the peer review board. The peer review board conducts an investigation and takes a vote. Typically, their decision is not final but constitutes a recommendation to management. Although you may think that employees will always back each other up, and managers will do the same, that is not the case. In general, members of the panel act impartially. The peer review process is especially useful as a final step for employee grievances, that is, in allowing the employee to make a final appeal. Employees are quite likely to accept peer review as a fair system because their own peers are involved.

To work well, regardless of which approach is used, grievance procedures must be communicated to employees and used in a consistent manner. Fortunately, according to one survey, grievance procedures are used infrequently, but, when they are used, are successful in providing a channel to air problems (Lo Bosco, 1985).

Fig. 2-6 SAMPLE GRIEVANCE FORM

EMPLOYEE GRIEVANCE FORM

Employee Name _____

Employee Position _____ Department _____

Employee's Supervisor _____

First Step. You are asked to speak informally with your immediate supervisor to try to settle the matter in a prompt and reasonable manner.

Second Step. If the first step does not produce satisfaction, you are asked to make a statement of your grievance in the space below. Include all facts giving rise to the grievance, including the date and individuals involved. Also explain what was not satisfactory about your supervisor's handling of this grievance. Then hand this form in to your immediate supervisor, who will arrange a meeting for the two of you and the department head within 10 working days. This grievance must be handed in within 7 days of the incident that gave rise to the grievance.

_____

_____

_____

_____

_____

_____

_____

_____

_____

_____   _____
         Employee Signature   Date

Date of receipt by supervisor: _____ Initials _____

Date of second-step meeting: _____

Meeting results: _____

_____

_____

_____

Fig. 2-6   Continued

Third Step. If you are not satisfied with the result of the second-step meeting, you can submit this grievance form to the director of human resources within 7 days of the meeting. The director will review your grievance and conduct a hearing within 10 working days of its receipt.

Date of receipt by the Director of Human Resources: _____   Initials: _____
Date of third-step meeting: _____
Meeting results: _____

_____
_____
_____
_____
_____
_____
_____

Fourth Step. If you are not satisfied with the result of the third-step meeting, you are asked to discuss with the director of human resources your choices for a final appeal. You must do so within 7 days of the third-step meeting.

Date of receipt by the Director of Human Resources: ____   Initials: _____
Date and mechanism of final appeal: _____

_____
_____

Results: _____

_____
_____
_____
_____
_____
_____
_____
_____

Communicating Expectations

Performance standards are generally communicated during orientation and training. It is best for them to be stated directly on the job description and/or performance appraisal form which are handed out during orientation.

Your operation's code of conduct can be circulated to new and current employees in an employee handbook. For union members, it will probably be included in the union contract. Whether the code of conduct is part of the employee handbook or delivered separately, new employees should be asked to sign upon receipt of their copies. The code of conduct should be reviewed with new hires during orientation and reviewed with all employees at least annually, both as a general reminder and to allow for employees' questions. The reason for the guidelines should be explained as employees are much more likely to follow rules when they know why those rules are important. It is also a good idea to post your rules of conduct in a highly visible location.

3

Dealing with Performance Issues

Evaluation of job performance is much more than an annual performance appraisal. It is a managerial function and responsibility and is the key to retaining, utilizing, and developing employees. Companies who realize this have replaced performance appraisal programs with performance management programs. In addition to reviewing performance at specific intervals (traditionally once a year), performance management programs stress ongoing coaching of employees (Fig. 3-1). As a result, the yearly performance appraisal is more likely to be effective because performance is monitored more closely during the year. Table 3-1 compares key aspects of performance management and performance appraisal.

This chapter discusses how to use coaching and performance appraisals to improve employee performance. At the end of the chapter there is a discussion on how to use performance appraisals at any time during the year (not just when they are regularly to be done) to set goals and time frames for the marginal employee who may face termination if performance is not improved. Before focusing on the specifics of coaching and performance appraisals, it can be helpful to consider two different kinds of skills that can make you more successful in these areas: active listening skills and skills to reduce employee defensiveness.

Listening Skills

One of the keys to successful coaching and performance appraisal is listening.

Fig. 3-1 PERFORMANCE MANAGEMENT CYCLE

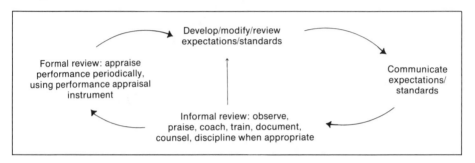

Guidelines for Active Listening

- Whenever possible, try to speak privately with your employees in an environment conducive to listening and free from distractions such as telephone calls and other interruptions.
- Whether your conversation concerns discipline, evaluation of performance, or most other topics, it is best to state the purpose of the meeting and then let the employee tell his or her own story first.
- The most basic guideline to keep in mind for active listening is that it is impossible to listen and talk at the same time. In other words, be quiet! You cannot be listening very well if you are interrupting the employee to get your thoughts across. So keep quiet, relax, and listen to the speaker until it is an appropriate time to speak.
- Show the employee you are trying to listen by maintaining good eye contact, leaning slightly forward, nodding your head affirmatively, using verbal expressions such as "yes" or "go on" to show interest, and standing or sitting close to the employee—without violating his or her personal space. Be relaxed. Smile.
- Concentrate your attention on what the employee is saying. Train yourself to focus on the emotions, feelings, and intent of the employee, as well as on the words. Ignore distractions such as kitchen noises.
- Listen for the employee's main ideas, such as specific concerns or needs, which may or may not be obvious from the conversation.

**Table 3-1 Comparison of Performance Appraisal
and Performance Management**

	Performance Appraisal	*Performance Management*
Atmosphere	Confrontational	Supportive
Time focus	The past	The future
Emphasis	The form	The process
Goal	Evaluation	Planning and achieving
Role of manager	Judge	Coach
Role of employee	Passive	Partner
Theme	Control	Sharing
Timing	Yearly	Ongoing
Criteria	Determined by management	Influenced by employees
Plan for development	Often omitted	Important part of process

Ask yourself, "Do I know for certain what he (she) means?" Listen for unspoken meanings behind the words.

▪ React to the ideas, not to the employee. Always maintain the self-respect and self-esteem of the employee.

▪ Do not jump to conclusions or make snap judgments. Suspend judgment and listen objectively.

▪ Keep your emotions in line. Emotions, particularly anger, limit your ability to listen.

▪ Try to see what the employee is saying from his or her point of view. You might find that what the employee is saying is not such a bad idea, even though you do not like it initially.

▪ Do not close your mind to information that is new, hard to understand, or complex.

▪ Do not discount an entire message because of disagreement with one point.

▪ Get the employee to tell you more by making statements such as "Tell me about it," "Let's discuss it," or "I would be interested in what you have to say."

▪ If when listening to an employee, you find that you cannot give an immediate answer, be sure to reply as soon as possible. This is crucial because, otherwise, the employee will feel forgotten, left out, or unimportant.

Reducing Employee Defensiveness

Evaluative situations, such as coaching and performance appraisal reviews, can easily generate employee defensiveness. Unfortunately, when an employee perceives a threat to his or her self-concept, he or she may react defensively, effectively blocking free and open communication. Signs of employee defensiveness include crossed arms, narrowed eyes, clenched hands, or body hunched forward.

To prevent this reaction, you need to create a nonthreatening, supportive climate in which to discuss performance. This can be done primarily by showing empathy and maintaining the employee's self-respect. The following techniques can help.

Strategies for Reducing Employee Defensiveness

- Focus on the behavior, not the employee.
- Make positive statements about the employee at the same time that you mention something that needs improvement.
- Let the employee know how important you think his or her job is, and that you know it can be really hectic.
- Make "I" statements instead of "you" statements. For example, instead of saying, "Your forgetfulness last night cost us some new customers," try, "I was really sorry to lose those new customers because I think we all work hard at getting new people in the door."
- Treat your employees as adults, not children.
- Do not act like a judge and jury. Your job is to help the employee improve.

If an employee perceives that you regard him or her with empathy and respect, the judgmental nature of your message can be neutralized.

Coaching

Coaching is a two-part process involving observation of employee performance and conversation focusing on job performance, between the manager and the employee. It is different from counseling, a process used to help employees who are performing poorly because of personal problems such as alcohol abuse (see Chapter 6). Coaching can take place informally at the employee's work station or in more formal coaching sessions in an office.

The overall goals of coaching are to evaluate work performance, and then to encourage optimum work performance by either reinforcing good performance or confronting and redirecting poor performance. Coaching, therefore, provides your employees with regular feedback and support about their job performance and helps you to understand exactly what your employees need to know. Coaching also shows your employees you care and prevents small problems from turning into big ones that may require much more attention later.

If coaching employees is so beneficial, why do managers often avoid it? Following are some possible reasons.

- Lack of time (In most cases, coaching requires only a few minutes.)
- Fear of confronting an employee with a concern about his or her performance (A mistake—the problem not faced may only get worse, not better.)
- Assumption that the employee already knows he or she is doing a good job—why bother saying anything? (Your employee would love to hear it anyway.)
- Little experience either doing or observing coaching (You can start practicing now.)
- Assumption that the employee will ask questions when appropriate and does not need feedback (Many employees are too proud or shy to ask questions.)

INFORMAL COACHING

The first step in coaching is to observe employees doing their jobs. *If an employee is doing the job well,* do not hesitate to tell him or her. All of us like to be told that we are doing a good job, so praise employees as often as you can. Work on catching your employees doing things right, and then use these steps.

1. Describe the specific action you are praising.
2. Explain the results or effects of the actions.
3. State your appreciation. Say thank you.

In some cases, you may want to write a letter of thanks and make sure that a copy goes into the employee's personnel file (Fig. 3-2). You could instead use a standard form (Fig. 3-3), which is quicker to complete.

If there appears to be a problem with some aspect of the employee's performance and you can correct it quickly, do so. Just be careful not to

Fig. 3-2   LETTER OF THANKS TO EMPLOYEE

Thank-You Memorandum
_____

TO: Tony Smith, Dishwasher
FROM: Tom Jones, Manager
DATE: 7/12/91

   Thank you for doing such a great job last night when the dishwasher broke down during the dinner rush. You very calmly informed your supervisor so a phone call could be made immediately to the repair company. Then you set up the three-compartment sink correctly and continued washing dishes until the job was done. Thanks for using your head and making sure the job was done right. We all appreciate what you did!

cc: Personnel file

correct one employee in front of another, as no one likes being corrected in front of his or her peers. Be sure, also, to correct the employee in a positive manner by saying, for instance, "That dish looks good—it could look even better if the garnish were a little fresher."

FORMAL COACHING

   If an employee needs more than a minor correction that informal coaching provides, or your minor corrections are not producing any results, you need to sit down and talk with the employee. Before doing so, think about following questions.

   Does the employee know what is supposed to be done and why?
   Does the employee know how it is supposed to be done?
   Are there any hindrances to the employee's performance that the employee cannot control, such as inadequate equipment? Is the performance standard realistic?
   Does the employee have a temporary personal problem?
   How serious are the consequences of this problem?
   Has the employee received feedback about this problem before, or has the problem been ignored?

Fig. 3-3   STANDARD RECOGNITION MEMO

MEMO

TO: _____

FROM: _____

DATE: _____

SUBJECT: POSITIVE PERFORMANCE

Describe employee's positive performance:

_____

_____

_____

_____

Thank you for being such a positive performer! We appreciate your efforts!

cc: Employee's file

The next step is to confront, not criticize, the employee's poor performance. Confronting is a positive process used to correct performance problems, gain the employee's commitment to improvement, and maintain a constructive supervisor-employee relationship. Criticism, on the other hand, is a negative process which, instead of concentrating on performance, blames the employee personally for not doing a job properly. It tends to be general, rather than specific, in nature and generates excuses, blaming of others, and guilt on the employee's part. Managers who confront employees are more interested in helping them feel confident about improving future performance, rather than making them feel inadequate and guilty about past performance.

When confronting an employee with what is perceived to be a performance problem, follow these steps.

1. Speak in private with the employee without any interruptions or distractions. Make the atmosphere as relaxed and friendly as possible.
2. Explain the reason for the meeting and express in a calm manner your concern about the specific aspect of job performance you

feel needs to be improved. Do so in a positive, caring manner. Describe the job performance concern in behavioral terms and explain its effect.

3. Ask the employee for his or her thoughts and opinions, using the six questions previously listed as a starting point to get feedback.

4. If it is clear that the employee can take some action to resolve the problem, work on getting his or her agreement to do this.

5. Next, ask the employee for some possible solutions to the problem. Discuss together these solutions and mutually agree on a course of action and time frame. Ask the employee to restate what has been agreed upon to check on understanding. State your confidence in the employee's ability to turn the situation around.

6. Finally, schedule a follow-up meeting to assess progress.

General Coaching Guidelines

- Be specific about the employee's job performance.
- Actively listen to the employee. Be supportive. Do not let the conversation drift away to other issues or other employees. If the conversation starts to drift, make a statement such as, "Let's get back to the issue at hand."
- Focus on the employee's behavior, not the employee. Always maintain the self-respect and self-esteem of the employee. To reduce employee defensiveness, use "I" statements rather than "you" statements.
- Reinforce or confront job performance as soon as possible after observing it. However, if you are at all angry or upset, do not confront the employee until you have cooled down.
- Praise in public, correct in private. Employees are very sensitive about being told they are doing something wrong in front of their peers. Unless the error could have grave consequences, wait until you can at least take the employee aside long enough to tell him or her how to correct it.
- Explain the impact of the employee's job performance, whether satisfactory or unsatisfactory, on the work group and entire operation.
- Be a coach, not a drill sergeant. Do not stay constantly at a person's side, watching everything he or she does.
- Allot a segment of each day, perhaps 10 to 30 minutes long, just to walk around and coach employees.

HOW TO DOCUMENT COACHING SESSIONS

You can document coaching sessions in one of two ways: either by entering it in a logbook, such as a supervisor's logbook (Fig. 3-4), or by filling out an employee incident record (Fig. 3-5). An entry into either type of record should include

Date and place of coaching session
Topic discussed and summary

A copy of this documentation is not given to either the department of human resources or to the employee. It is strictly for your use in the event that the employee does not improve.

Performance Appraisal

Performance appraisal, the periodic evaluation of an employee's job performance, is one of the more negatively viewed and poorly performed of managerial tasks. Ron Zemke in *Training* magazine states, "Performance appraisals are about as beloved as IRS audits. . . . Evidence has been popping up to suggest that most performance appraisal systems are more noteworthy for the angst they create than the results they achieve." Managers and subordinates alike generally dislike performance appraisal programs and interviews. Managers often view the performance appraisal program as time-consuming (which it often is), are doubtful that positive results will follow, and hesitate telling employees that they have areas of improvement. Likewise, employees feel that they do not get a chance to say much (which is usually true), that the boss is not prepared, and that they are being evaluated unfairly, with an emphasis on the negative rather than the positive. Other areas of employee discontent are as follows:

Employees hate the idea that the appraisal is *done to* them.
Employees doubt that managers can make really accurate evaluations.
Employees do not like the evaluative tone.
Employees feel that the appraisal overemphasizes the past.
Employees do not think there is enough emphasis on personal development.

Figure 3-6 summarizes ways to make the performance appraisal

Fig. 3-4 SAMPLE OF SUPERVISOR'S LOG

		SUPERVISOR'S LOGBOOK	
Date	Time	Report of Problems, Counselings, etc.	Initials

Fig. 3-5 SAMPLE EMPLOYEE INCIDENT RECORD

EMPLOYEE INCIDENT RECORD

Employee Name _____   Title _____

Date of Employment _____   Department _____

Remember to sign and date all entries.

Date of Incident	Description of Incident (Include where it took place.)	Action Taken and When

Fig. 3-6 PERFORMANCE APPRAISAL GUIDELINES

HOW TO MAKE PERFORMANCE APPRAISAL MORE ACCEPTABLE TO EMPLOYEES

1. Focus on developing employees, rather than simply evaluating employees.
2. Emphasize future achievement, rather than just past performance.
3. Make the mutual establishment of work goals an important part of the process.
4. Make the employee a partner in the process, instead of the receiver.
5. Give employees feedback frequently during the year.
6. Allow employees to be involved in the process of developing the performance appraisal form.

---

process more acceptable to employees and, at the same time, a more valuable process.

Performance appraisals have various roles or uses in foodservice operations. A performance appraisal lets the employee get an answer to the question "How well am I doing?" This is not only an opportunity for the employee to get feedback on how well he or she is meeting standards, but also for both employee and supervisor to communicate other performance concerns. If problem areas of work performance are identified, the employee may be advised to undergo training. Very often, the performance appraisal acts as the basis for an employee's salary increase (referred to as pay for performance) and possible promotion. Opportunities for career and personal development can be discussed at this time. When done in an appropriate manner, performance appraisals can also enhance employees' satisfaction and motivation.

For the organization, performance appraisals are used to improve communication and manager-employee relationships, remind employees of the company's goals and missions, determine training needs, and improve performance. These outcomes may then lead to increased morale and decreased employee turnover.

PERFORMANCE APPRAISAL FORMS

Some performance appraisal systems simply use performance standards against which performance will be measured (Fig. 3-7). Performance standards are discussed in Chapter 2.

Another popular way to evaluate employees uses the graphic rating scale. Figure 3-8 depicts one that, though still often used, has some serious handicaps. In its left-hand column are performance dimensions, such as job knowledge and quality of work. To the right are the rating or response categories, such as Outstanding or Satisfactory.

Performance dimensions are often based on personality traits considered important to good job performance, such as dependability, communication, and cooperation. The use of such traits in job evaluations should be avoided unless they can be defined in terms of observable, job-related behavior. For instance, "dependability" can be rephrased as "comes to work on time."

Another problem with this graphic rating scale example is that the rating categories are quite vague and ambiguous and could be interpreted quite differently by two different raters. Rating categories should be behaviorally based, unambiguous, and relevant to the dimensions being rated. For example, response categories for the performance dimension "ability to adjust and use recipes" may range from "employee accurately adjusts recipes and follow instructions precisely" to "employee frequently makes errors adjusting and following recipes." These categories have much more meaning and can be used more accurately by reviewers. In general, five to nine response categories produce the most consistent ratings.

In addition to evaluating performance, appraisal forms should also have a section in which future work goals are mutually formulated during the performance appraisal interview. Thus, the appraisal does not consider only prior performance, but also looks ahead and allows the employee to be involved in developing the goals by which he will be evaluated next time.

To be used successfully, performance appraisal forms also need to be

Easy to understand and use
Acceptable to the evaluators
Acceptable to the employees (They should be involved in development of such forms.)
Explained to employees during orientation
Reviewed and revised periodically

RATING ERRORS

The rater or evaluator has the responsibility of rating an employee's performance and communicating this rating to the employee. Raters should receive training in both these areas, as they both require certain skills. Common rating errors include the following:

Fig. 3-7 PERFORMANCE APPRAISAL FORM

SERVER PERFORMANCE EVALUATION

Name: _____

Position: _____

Date of Hire: _____ Yearly or 60-Day Evaluation: _____

Department: _____

Please use COMMENT section whenever "Exceeds" or "Does Not Meet" is checked. POINTS: Exceeds—5, Meets—3, Does not meet—0.

Performance Standards	Exceeds	Meets	Does Not Meet
1. Stocks the service station for one serving area for one meal completely and correctly, as specified on the Service Station Procedures Sheet, in 10 minutes or less.	_____ Comments:	_____	_____
2. Sets or resets a table properly, as shown on the Table Setting Layout Sheet, in not more than 3 minutes.	_____ Comments:	_____	_____
3. Greets guests cordially within 5 minutes after they are seated and takes their order if time permits; if too busy, informs them that he or she will be back as soon as possible.	_____ Comments:	_____	_____
4. Explains menu to customers: accurately describes the day's specials and, if asked, accurately answers any questions on portion size, ingredients, taste, and preparation method.	_____ Comments:	_____	_____

Fig. 3-7 Continued

Performance Standards	Exceeds	Meets	Does Not Meet
5. Takes food, wine, and beverage orders accurately and legibly for a table of up to six guests according to Guest Check Procedures; prices and totals check with 100 percent accuracy. Comments:	_____	_____	_____
6. Picks up order and completes plate preparation according to Plate Preparation Procedure. Comments:	_____	_____	_____
7. Serves a complete meal to all persons at each table in an assigned station in not more than 1 hour per table using the Tray Service Procedures. Comments:	_____	_____	_____
8. If asked, recommends wines appropriate to menu items selected, according to the What Wine Goes with What Food Sheet; opens and serves wines correctly as shown on the Wine Service Sheet. Comments:	_____	_____	_____
9. Accepts and processes payment with 100 percent accuracy as specified on the Check Payment Procedures Sheet. Comments:	_____	_____	_____
10. Performs side work correctly according to the Side Work Assignments Sheet and as requested. Comments:	_____	_____	_____
11. Operates all equipment in assigned area according to the Safety Manual. Comments:	_____	_____	_____

Supervision in the Hospitality Industry, Jack E. Miller and Mary Porter. Copyright © 1985 by Jack E. Miller and Mary Porter. Reprinted by permission of John Wiley & Sons, Inc.

Fig. 3-7 Continued

Performance Standards	Exceeds	Meets	Does Not Meet
12. Meets at all times the Dress Code requirements. Comments:	_____	_____	_____
13. Uses at all times the sanitation procedures specified for serving personnel in the Sanitation Manual; maintains work area to score 90 percent or higher on the Sanitation Checklist. Comments:	_____	_____	_____
14. Maintains a "Good" or higher rating on the Customer Relations Checklist; maintains a customer complaint ratio of less than 1 per 200 customers served. Comments:	_____	_____	_____
15. Maintains a check average of not less than $7 per person at lunch and $15 per person at dinner. Comments:	_____	_____	_____
16. Is absent from work less than 12 days in a year. Comments:	_____	_____	_____
17. Is late to work less than 12 times in a year. Comments:	_____	_____	_____
18. Can always be found in work area during work hours or supervisor knows where he or she is. Comments:	_____	_____	_____
19. Attends or makes up all required meetings and training. Comments:	_____	_____	_____
20. Supervisor receives positive feedback from peers with minimal complaints Comments:	_____	_____	_____

Fig. 3-7 **Continued**

OVERALL RATING:

Outstanding Performance: 75–100 points (must meet or exceed all standards)

Good Performance: 50–74 points

Marginal Performance, Reevaluate in 60 Days: Below 50 points

EVALUATOR'S COMMENTS: _____

_____

_____

EMPLOYEE'S COMMENTS: Please comment freely on this evaluation.

_____

_____

_____

EMPLOYEE'S OBJECTIVES: What would you like to accomplish in the next 12 months? _____

_____

_____

EMPLOYEE'S OBJECTIVES FOR THE NEXT 12 MONTHS:

(Plan should be specific, realistic, measurable, and include target dates.)

_____

_____

_____

SIGNATURES:

_____   _____   _____
Employee   Evaluator   Reviewer
Date:_____

Fig. 3-8 GRAPHIC RATING SCALE

Factors	Unsatisfactory	Conditional	Average	Above Average	Outstanding
Quality of work					
Quantity of work					
Job knowledge					
Cooperation					
Dependability					
Attendance					
Appearance					
Get along with others					

A major error related to rating employee performance is making *subjective evaluations.* Being objective is difficult, because each evaluator brings to the rating process his or her own attitudes, values, perceptions, prejudices, stereotypes, and emotions. Objective evaluation starts with appraising an employee's performance, not the employee.

The *halo effect* refers to allowing the rating of one aspect of performance in which an employee does very well, such as being cooperative, to influence positively the rating of other aspects. For example, a cook who does very well in the area of practicing good sanitation and always has a neat, clean appearance, might also be rated highly on his ability to produce high quality food, which may not be the case. The opposite of the halo effect is the *horns effect,* by which a poor rating in one aspect of the evaluation negatively influences the rating of other factors.

The *error of central tendency* occurs when evaluators tend to rate everyone about the same because of an inclination to avoid extremes when rating anything. Typically, employees may be ranked as average or just above average.

Leniency error occurs when the evaluator is too generous with the ratings as a result of a tendency to want to be everyone's friend and to avoid the unpleasant tasks of confronting and discussing performance problems and dealing with employee defensiveness. Evaluators inflate ratings for other reasons as well: to avoid confronting poor performance with hard-to-manage employees, to help someone whose work performance is declining because of personal problems, to make the department look good, to make sure an employee gets a decent raise, or to encourage an employee whose performance is poor overall, but who has made much progress prior to the appraisal. One problem with leniency is that when performance slips and an employee is fired, the employee, if he or she takes the decision to court, could win the case when his or her many "good" evaluations are brought to light. Another problem with leniency is that if employees are never told of their deficiencies, their performance and productivity may not improve and they are thus less likely to be promoted. The opposite of leniency error is *severity error*, by which everyone is rated poorly. This may occur when the rater is a perfectionist and few employees measure up to his or her tough interpretation of the performance standards.

Recency error occurs when the employee is rated only on his or her most recent performance. Performance review does not begin a month before the yearly review session, but actually starts a full year earlier. Recency error frequently occurs because the rater has insufficient and/or erroneous documentation of employee performance, so that only vague, general statements based on recent observations are written. This upsets the employee especially when incidents of outstanding performance are forgotten. Some employees are aware that the boss reviews only recent performance, so they save their energy and work diligently just during the last part of the appraisal period.

First impression and fixed impression errors both refer to a rater who has limited insight into an employee's performance. In first impression error, the evaluator rates an employee solely on his or her first impression of the employee, and not on subsequent performance. In fixed impression error, the evaluator typically bases an employee's performance on only a few observations, which then form the basis for evaluation.

In addition to these rating errors, length of service can affect ratings significantly. It is often difficult for an evaluator to give an employee a less than satisfactory rating after many years of satisfactory and/or previous good ratings.

When evaluating an employee's performance, do the following:

Evaluate the performance, not the employee. Be objective.
Give specific examples of performance to back up ratings.
Where there is substandard performance, ask, "Why?" Use the rule of finger, which means pointing (looking closely) at yourself before pointing at (blaming) the employee. Perhaps the employee

was not given enough training or the appropriate tools to do the job.

Think about fairness and consistency when evaluating performance. Ask yourself, "If this were my review, how would I react?"

Get input from others who have some working relationship with the employee.

Write down some ideas to discuss with the employee on how to improve performance.

EMPLOYEE SELF-APPRAISAL

As part of some performance appraisal systems, employees are asked to fill out a performance appraisal and evaluate themselves. Self-appraisal is surprisingly accurate. Many tend to underrate themselves, particularly the better employees, whereas less effective employees may overrate themselves. If an employee is given the chance to participate, and the manager really reads and takes the self-appraisal seriously, the employee gets the message that his or her opinion matters. This may result in less employee defensiveness and a more constructive performance appraisal interview. It may also improve motivation and job performance. Self-appraisal is particularly justified when an employee works largely without supervision.

THE PERFORMANCE APPRAISAL INTERVIEW

The performance appraisal interview is a time to give encouragement and work on improving performance and building commitment to the organization. This is a time to help and develop employees, not to punish or simply evaluate past performance.

If the appraisal interview is conducted only once a year, it is probably too late to give praise or remedy most problems that occurred during the past year. Unfortunately, many annual performance appraisals have salary review as their major purpose and function. Whether happy or unhappy with the ratings, the employee tends not to focus on the evaluation as much as on the increase. It is best to do two performance appraisals a year, 6 months apart, one for performance review and one for salary administration. In addition, a performance appraisal should be done at the end of the probationary period of a new employee. Keep in mind that preparation is an integral part of the appraisal interview.

Guidelines for Preparation

▪ In advance, explain thoroughly the performance appraisal instrument and interview process to the employee.
▪ If employees are asked to do self-evaluations, ask the employee to complete his or her form. Self-evaluation is a wonderful way to make the employee more of a doer than a receiver in this process. Explain that his or her feedback is important in this process and request the employee to fill out the form as completely and honestly as possible.
▪ Set an appropriate time for the interview that is convenient for the employee. Do not do appraisals during the employee's break time. Select a place to hold the interview that is quiet and informal and where there will be no interruptions. Some employees find the boss's office to be threatening or intimidating, so you may want to choose a neutral location. Tell the employee where and when.
▪ Review the entire file and fill out the performance appraisal form, using the employee's self-evaluation if you have it.
▪ You may want to give the employee a copy of your completed performance appraisal a day or so before the interview. This allows the employee time to really read and think about the evaluation as well as to develop responses.

Guidelines for a Performance Appraisal Interview

▪ Establish and maintain a friendly, relaxed, and trusting atmosphere by
    Sitting with the employee side by side
    Maintaining good eye contact
    Explaining that honesty and feedback are important and that the discussion will be on performance, not personality
    Starting with a statement of purpose and agenda
    Reading employee nonverbal language for tension, anxiety, and misunderstanding
    Using positive, constructive language instead of negative language; for instance, using "concern" instead of "problem," "growth" instead of "shortcoming"
    Actively listening
    Being a coach instead of a judge
    Being constructive with your criticism
    Giving specific examples and avoiding generalities
    Not allowing the conversation to drift to unrelated areas

- Using the performance appraisal form (do not read directly from it!), start with a discussion of employee strengths and give praise.
- Next, identify and ask for feedback on areas that need improvement. Be sure to cite specific examples of poor performance.
- If the employee disagrees with your assessment of problem areas, listen and be open-minded enough to allow him or her to change your mind. The employee may let you know of situations of which you were not previously aware. Be prepared to change your evaluation if you feel you should.
- After identifying areas in which the employee needs to improve, help him or her to develop a plan of action to build on performance strengths and overcome weaknesses. Make sure this plan has deadlines and is specific, realistic, measurable, consistent with company policy, and understood by the employee. Provide direction for the future.
- Show the employee you are genuinely concerned about his or her performance by asking if there is anything you can do to help, and if there is anything you are doing that makes it difficult for the employee to do his or her job.
- Summarize and conclude on a positive note, for example, by telling the employee how important his or her contribution is to the organization.
- Ask the employee to sign the written evaluation, making any comments as appropriate. Be sure to give the employee a copy.

USING PERFORMANCE APPRAISALS WITH THE MARGINAL EMPLOYEE

When an employee is unable, after repeated coaching, to meet performance standards or expectations, the best approach is to do a performance review or appraisal. If the situation arises at the time of year when reviews are usually given, so much the better. If not, do not hesitate to go through the performance review process anyway. By documenting and discussing problem areas with the employee, together you can set up performance goals and time frames, such as 30, 60, or 90 days, for reaching the agreed-upon goals. You now have documentation, including the employee's signature, stating what the consequences will be if performance goals are not met (Fig. 3-9). Figure 3-10 is a performance improvement checklist that you can use to ensure that all necessary actions are taken.

Performance problems can be used as the basis for a nondisciplinary termination. In the event that you are considering terminating an employee for poor performance, make sure you have done the following:

Based your evaluation of unsatisfactory job performance on standardized, objective, and job-related evaluation techniques

Given the employee a reasonable amount of time to meet performance objectives

Made a reasonable effort and reasonable accommodations to help the employee meet performance standards (For instance, you should do more to accommodate a long-term employee with a previous satisfactory record than a new employee.)

Given the employee a chance to appeal performance appraisal findings

Documented clearly that the employee did not meet objectives in follow-up evaluations

These steps are particularly important to avoid wrongful discharge suits.

Fig. 3-9   SAMPLE NOTICE—SECTION OF PERFORMANCE APPRAISAL OF THE MARGINAL EMPLOYEE

NOTICE

___X___   Your performance appraisal rating is UNSATISFACTORY. Your performance must be brought up to "Satisfactory" during the next 60-day period. During this time you will be on probation. If at the end of this period you have not achieved the results you set below with your supervisor, you may be terminated.

Employee's Plan for Work Improvement:

Area	Description of Required Results	How Satisfactory Results Will Be Measured
1		
2		
3		
4		
5		

Signatures:

Employee _____   Date _____

Supervisor _____   Date _____

General Manager _____   Date _____

Human Resources _____   Date _____

Fig. 3-10   SAMPLE PERFORMANCE IMPROVEMENT CHECKLIST

PERFORMANCE IMPROVEMENT CHECKLIST

Establishing Goals

_____   1. Have specific areas been identified in which the employee needs to improve?

_____   2. Have you met with the employee to discuss and mutually agree on how the employee can best improve in each area?

_____   3. Have specific goals that seem realistic and reasonable been agreed upon?

_____   4. Have you agreed on a date by which these goals will be met?

_____   5. Have you also agreed on an interim date to check progress?

_____   6. Have all details been documented?

_____   7. Has the employee signed the document?

_____   8. Has the employee been made aware, in speaking and in writing, of the consequences if he or she does not meet the goals?

Reviewing Progress

_____   9. Are you regularly checking with the employee to see how he or she is progressing?

_____   10. Are you coaching the employee when appropriate?

Checking Results

_____   11. Has the employee successfully met all the objectives?

_____   12. If so, have you thought of ways to ensure that performance does not slip again?

_____   13. If not, go through termination procedures unless there are extenuating circumstances.

4

Dealing with Violations of Conduct Rules

The procedure for dealing with most violations of conduct rules is basically the same: fact-finding, the disciplinary interview, and, if matters are not resolved in the interview, decision making and implementation of the decision. Each step is discussed in detail in this chapter.

Fact-Finding

When an undesirable incident occurs, for instance, if a customer complains about terrible service, do not rush to do something, such as writing up a corrective action warning, until you have a good idea of what happened and have considered the employee's background. Even if you witnessed the incident, you will need more information before you can make any type of disciplinary decision. It can be very embarrassing to pronounce a certain employee guilty, without documentation in hand, only to find out that the particular employee was off on the day in question. Therefore, do your fact-finding first, and do it in a timely manner. Get the facts; do not draw conclusions; they can come later. Remember that an employee is innocent until proven guilty.

Use the following questions to guide you.

1. *Evidence*—Is there enough evidence to justify action? What are the sources of the evidence? Is there direct or only indirect evidence of employee guilt?
2. *Extentuating circumstances*—Was the problem caused largely by a situation beyond the employee's control? Does the employee have a temporary personal problem? Was the employee provoked by a manager or another employee?

3. *Employee's understanding of the rules*—Did the employee understand the rules or procedures and the consequences for failing to follow them?
4. *Employee's past performance and work record*—Is this the first problem you have had with this employee, or one of many? Has the same problem occurred previously? How was it handled? How long has the employee worked here?
5. *Seriousness of the problem*—What type of infraction is this? How seriously does it impact on the operation? Are you making a moral judgment or a business judgment?
6. *Willful misconduct*—Was the action deliberate?
7. *Past practice*—How have similar problems been handled? Have corrective actions been consistently enforced?

When reviewing the employee's employment record, include recent performance evaluations and documentation of any prior problems. Discuss this person's performance and work record with any other managers who are familiar with the employee, as well as human resource managers, as appropriate in your company. Be sure to consider an employee's overall record and contributions.

Disciplinary Interview

As part of your investigation, you need to confront the employee with the incident from the perspective of concern. Unfortunately, this part of the discipline process is commonly mishandled, resulting in the employee's being denied due process. Mishandling may be due to any of the following shortcomings.

- The manager has his or her mind made up and, perhaps, even a disciplinary notice already written up as the interview begins. The message is delivered to the employee in a one-way conversation, and any questioning or confrontation by the employee is obviously unwanted (and probably feared) by the manager.
- All the facts obtained by the manager are not revealed (probably because they were not documented) or are purposely concealed (probably to trick the employee into disclosing some information).
- Instead of a supportive, caring interview in which the employee feels that someone will listen to his or her side, the individual is outnumbered (there are two managers present), and it is obvious that the managers have their minds made up. It is little wonder the employee feels intimidated, embarrassed, and resentful and does not try to defend him- or herself.

Of key importance during this discussion is to begin with an open mind and to talk calmly and in a nonthreatening manner with the employee. Another way to help an employee get a fair hearing is to let him or her bring another person to the disciplinary interview. If an employee requests representation during a disciplinary interview, you should allow it.

Following are steps and guidelines for conducting disciplinary interviews.

1. Decide on when and where you will meet with the employee. Never discuss a problem when either you or the employee is upset about it, as your discussion will not be very productive. Likewise, do not wait too long to have this discussion; justice delayed is justice denied. Pick a spot that is private. If you choose your office, make arrangements so that you are not interrupted. Do not let anything in your office distract you. You will fail to show your employee your genuine concern for improvement if you do not give him or her your full attention.

2. Avoid small talk and get down to business right away. Open the conversation by saying, for example, "I am very concerned about something that happened in the kitchen last night, and I would like to take a few minutes to discuss it with you. I first want to present you with what I know, and then I want to hear your side of the story." Use nonverbal language to show concern. For example, do not sit behind a desk; instead sit next to the employee. Do not cross your arms; that shows defensiveness.

3. Next, go over the facts with the employee. Be specific about times, places, actions, and any other details. If you blame the employee personally or make generalities such as "You always do this," you should not be surprised if you come face to face with an angry, defensive employee. Do not worry about assigning blame; instead think about solutions. Also explain the impact of the consequences of the employee's actions, such as the possibility of guests becoming ill from food-borne bacteria when the cook leaves frozen chicken out at room temperature to defrost.

4. Tell the employee that he or she is a valuable employee and that you would like his or her explanation of what happened. Actively listen and get all the details. Do not disagree or argue with the employee even though you may feel like interrupting. Be quiet and work on understanding what the employee is telling you. Show the employee you are listening by maintaining good eye contact, leaning slightly forward, nodding your

head affirmatively, and using verbal expressions such as "yes" or "go on" to show interest.

5. Try to reach a mutual understanding about what happened and why it happened. If it seems that you and the employee agree on these points, based on your discussion up to this point, summarize what went wrong. If there is no agreement, end the meeting, explaining to the employee that you will have to decide what action, if any, will be taken.

6. Next, ask the employee for some solutions to the problem by saying, for example, "What do you think you can do so that this doesn't happen again?" Your role here is to help the employee identify some possible solutions; it is not for you to impose or take responsibility for any particular solution. Help the employee to identify several different solutions so that he or she does not see a solution that you suggested as the only possibility. Because it is the employee who must live with the solution, let the employee select the one he or she feels will work best. Decide on a time frame and set a date when you will meet again to discuss progress.

7. If this discussion constitutes a step in your progressive action system, inform the employee of such, as well as what the next step will be if there is no improvement.

8. If a written discipline notice is being used, complete the notice and ask the employee and any witnesses to sign it. Be sure to inform the employee clearly that signing the documentation signifies only his or her understanding of, not agreement with, what is stated. If an employee refuses to sign, write on the notice, "Refused to sign." Include the date and time, and initial the note. In addition, the employee should also be advised of the grievance procedure, if one exists, and invited to make written comments on the form.

9. Close by asking the employee to restate what has been agreed upon, to check on understanding. State your confidence in the employee's ability to turn the situation around and tell him or her how much you genuinely want to see improvement. Finally, stress that if the employee is having trouble resolving the problem, he or she is to speak with you as soon as possible.

10. Document the entire discussion. Documentation will be discussed in detail in a following section of this chapter.

Make a note on your calendar to follow up this discussion by checking on the situation after a reasonable interval.

Decision Making and Implementation of the Decision

If you were not able to come to an agreement with the employee as to the nature of the problem, you need to review and examine carefully the evidence discussed with the employee and his or her defense before making a decision. Any factual disputes should be resolved before disciplinary action is taken. Using the seven questions in the fact-finding step, decide whether disciplinary action is appropriate and, if so, what kind. If you decide to take disciplinary action, discuss the following with the employee.

▪ A review of the incident, including the results of the investigation
▪ The disciplinary decision

Then proceed to cover steps 6 to 10 in the guidelines for disciplinary interviews.

If you decide not to take action, inform the employee as soon as possible. It is not fair to keep the employee guessing about such an important matter.

Documentation

For many managers, documenting disciplinary actions is an unwelcome chore. It is time-consuming, and there always seem to be more important things to do. Why the insistence on documentation? There are some very good reasons. Documentation is necessary

To provide evidence should you ever be sued, taken to an unemployment hearing, or receive a grievance
To help the manager clarify the facts and see the situation as objectively as possible
To help the employee improve

The first step in progressive discipline, a *verbal warning*, should be, despite its name, documented. A common misconception is that verbal warnings should be just that, verbal, and do not need to be recorded. In the event you ever find yourself at an unemployment hearing or in a similar situation, you will need documentation of this first step. A verbal warning can be documented in a supervisor's logbook (Fig. 4-1) or by using an employee incident record (Fig. 4-2). An entry into either type of record should include

**Fig. 4-1   SAMPLE OF VERBAL WARNING DOCUMENTATION IN
SUPERVISOR'S LOG**

SUPERVISOR'S LOGBOOK

Date	Time	Report Problems, Counselings, etc.	Initials
1/9/92	2:00 P.M.	Verbally warned Sally Price	ACD
		(cold food prep) not to leave	
		tuna fish salad at room	
		temperature for 2 hours as	
		she did today. She said	
		she forgot. I reminded her	
		that this has happened	
		more than once and that	
		it could cause people to	
		become very ill. I told	
		her next step is a written	
		warning.	

Date and place of incident
Topic discussed and summary

It is not usual to give a copy of this documentation to either the human resources office or the employee. It is for your own use in the event that the situation progresses to the next step. Any counseling regarding misconduct prior to this first step should also be recorded in the supervisor's logbook or the employee incident record.

The next steps in progressive discipline, written warning, suspension, and termination, are more serious and are normally documented on a form such as shown in Figure 4-3.

Guidelines for Documenting Disciplinary Action

- Document performance as quickly as possible, including the date(s).

Fig. 4-2 SAMPLE OF VERBAL WARNING DOCUMENTATION IN EMPLOYEE INCIDENT RECORD

EMPLOYEE INCIDENT RECORD

Employee Name John Jones Title Cook

Date of Employment 2/12/91 Department Food and Beverage

Remember to sign and date all entries.

Date of Incident	Description of Incident (Include where it took place)	Action Taken and When
2/20/92 6:15 P.M.	John was using 8 oz. ladle for seafood Newburg instead of 6 oz. ladle on serving line.	Reminded John immediately to check portion listing every night before serving. Told him this was a verbal warning and next step it will be a written warning. I explained that portion control is crucial to customer satisfaction and to keep costs down. ACD 2/21/92

67

- Be specific about what the employee did and the circumstances under which the behavior occurred. Make sure your notes are accurate and behavior-oriented. Document thoroughly by including who, what, when, where, and how.
- Explain briefly the impact or consequences of the employee's actions. Describe the significance of the behavior as compared with expected behavior.
- Opinions and hearsay have no place in documentation. Note only facts, behavior, and direct observation. Be objective and clear.
- Document all information revealed in the investigation, as well as that obtained from the employee during the interview.
- Document any corrective action taken, the employee's plan for improvement, and the follow-up date.
- Always note what the following step will be if the employee does not improve.

Administering Discipline

Perhaps the most important issue to employees is whether management is fair and consistent in taking corrective measures. In any disciplinary action, it is important to maintain the employee's respect and trust in management, as well as his or her own self-respect.

It is important, too, to act in a timely manner and to ensure that the disciplinary action is appropriate to the situation.

Guidelines for Administering Discipline

- To ensure fairness and consistency, consult with appropriate people, such as human resources representatives. Consistency is especially important as a deterrent. When employees know that they will be caught and disciplined for doing something wrong, they are less likely to do it.
- Always express concern for your employees. Be positive and supportive. State your confidence in the employee's ability to improve. Your job is to help the employee, not to harbor a grudge.
- To maintain the respect and trust of each of your employees, do not discuss one employee's performance with another during a disciplinary interview. This is strictly confidential. Employees commonly try to drag other employees' names into the discussion. When this happens, you need to make a statement such as, "Right now we are discussing your performance only. I am sure you would not want me to discuss your performance behind your back

Fig. 4-3 SAMPLE EMPLOYEE WARNING NOTICE

EMPLOYEE WARNING NOTICE

Employee Name _____
Position Title _____ Department _____
Date and Time of Incident _____

Type of Incident

_____ Excessive absenteeism/lateness   _____ Failure to
                                                           perform job
                                                           duties

_____ Abuse of break times/meal periods   _____ Sleeping on duty
_____ Neglect of safety rules   _____ Not fit for duty
_____ Improper dress   _____ Other: _____

Description of Incident (include results of investigation and employee
comments):

Previous warning(s): _____ Yes _____ No
If yes, give date(s) and type(s) of incident(s).

Employee Improvement Plan (include time frame for improvement):

Consequences If Improvement Does Not Occur:

_____

Action Taken: _____   Warning (Note first or second)
                   _____   Suspension   Date(s): _____
                   _____   Termination   Effective Date: _____
I have discussed the above with the employee on:

_____ _____ _____
  Date   Time   Supervisor's Signature

Employee Section
Comments: (If you disagree with the action taken or anything else, please
make comments in this space.)

Your signature means only that you have been advised of the contents of
this warning. It does not signify that you agree with its contents.

_____   _____
    Employee's Signature   Date

with another employee, so please don't ask me to do that to anyone else."

- Always maintain the self-respect and self-esteem of the employee. Remember that your concern is with the individual's actions, not the individual.
- Take corrective action in a timely manner to ensure effectiveness. However, if you are annoyed or angry, wait until you cool off. In circumstances when you must react quickly to an employee's actions, such as theft, the appropriate action is to suspend the employee pending an investigation. If the employee is found innocent, he or she must be compensated with full pay for all time lost.
- Keep an open mind until all the facts are in, including the employee's response.
- Balance corrective action with positive reinforcement. When employees do things right, write them a "thank-you" or recognition memo.
- Document, document, document.

5

Termination

Termination refers to an employee's leaving his or her position. Termination may be voluntary, commonly referred to as a *quit*, or involuntary, commonly referred to as a *discharge*. An employee may quit his or her position for many different reasons, such as retirement, promotion, or transfer. An employee can also leave for personal reasons (such as moving out of town), a chance to advance elsewhere, a career change, or dissatisfaction with some aspect of the employer-employee relationship. In some cases, employees simply abandon their jobs. An employee may be discharged for one of the following reasons.

- Unsatisfactory completion of probationary period
- Violation of a conduct rule
- Unsatisfactory work performance
- Layoff (reduction in work force)
- Elimination of position as a result of acquisition, sale, or reorganization of business

Termination has become an important issue because wrongful discharge suits are very costly. According to a 1988 survey, the average jury award to wrongfully discharged employees was approximately $600,000 and the most frequent award was $250,000. Former employees may be awarded with back pay, front pay (pay for the period of time it will take for the employee to get a comparable job), emotional distress damages, professional reputation damages, and punitive damages (based on severe misconduct by the employer).

This chapter discusses the employment at-will doctrine and just cause terminations, termination policy and procedures, alternatives to dismissal, guidelines for a just cause termination, and the termination interview.

Employment-at-Will and Just Cause

The relationship between employer and employee has long followed the *employment-at-will doctrine*. This doctrine states that either the employer or the employee is free to sever the employment relationship at any time, without notice or reason, as long as there is no employment contract requiring a specific duration of employment. In other words, you can fire employees on a whim and they would have absolutely no recourse.

The employment-at-will doctrine started to lose its significance with the passage of legislation, such as the Civil Rights Act of 1964, that prohibited employee termination based on race, color, sex, national origin, religion, age, pregnancy, or physical handicaps. Fairly recently, the courts in various states have made judgments that are continually eroding the employment-at-will doctrine, based on the following three theories.

- Public policy
- Implied employment contract
- Breach of good faith

Many courts have been making exceptions to the employment-at-will principle on the basis of public policy. What this means is that an employer may not terminate an employee for reasons that are in violation of public policy, such as the following:

Discharging an employee because of his or her obligation to perform jury service

Discharging for performing duties as a member of the National Guard

Discharging in retaliation for refusal to perform an illegal act on behalf of the employer

Discharging in retaliation for whistle-blowing concerning the illegal acts of the employer (such as making false statements)

Discharging an employee who is exercising a legal right, such as filing for workers' compensation

Discharging for participation in union activities or union-organizing efforts

Former employees have used verbal and written evidence in court to support the contention that there was an implied legally enforceable contract between themselves and their employers. An individual may focus on verbal promises of career employment made in an interview, payroll cards showing status as a permanent employee, or an employee handbook that implies job security. In some cases, despite the existence of written disclaimers explaining that employment is at-will, former employees have successfully shown that oral and/or written representations guaranteed them a job and have gone on to win their cases.

Employers have also lost lawsuits because they could not demonstrate that they acted in good faith. Specifically, they could not prove that the employee was given every reasonable chance to improve before being terminated.

Some employers are trying to protect their at-will prerogative by doing the following:

Avoiding references to "career" employment in recruiting and selecting

Asking job applicants to sign at-will statements (see Fig. 5-1)

Asking new hires to sign at-will statements (see Fig. 5-1)

Putting at-will statements into the employee handbook (see Fig. 5-1) that indicate that none of its provisions prevent the company from terminating employees at-will for any reason and at any time

Changing "permanent status" to "regular" or "full-time"

Avoiding oral or written statements promising any type of job security, such as "As long as you keep doing well, you will always have a job working here."

At this time it is safe to say that employment-at-will is on its way out, and there is a strong trend toward making it a requirement of law to discharge employees only for *just cause*. When you terminate an employee for just cause, the employee has received due process (see Chapter 1) and, as a result, fair treatment. The advantages of using the just cause approach to terminations are many. Because some job applicants will not sign at-will statements on applications, you will lose some potential employees. Of more importance is that the courts have never denied the right to dismiss an employee when that employee received due process and fair treatment. When employees believe that they have been granted due process, they seem less likely to file complaints or lawsuits of wrongful discharge or discrimination.

According to one author (Redeker, 1989), there are four good reasons that you should develop a discipline system based on due process and fair treatment.

"1. To create a productive, responsible work force committed to the enterprise;

Fig. 5-1 SAMPLE AT-WILL STATEMENTS

AT-WILL STATEMENTS

On Job Application:

I understand that this employment application and any other company documents are not contracts of employment and that any individual who is hired may voluntarily leave employment upon proper notice and may be terminated by the company at any time and for any reason. I understand that no employee of the company has the authority to make any agreement to the contrary, and I acknowledge that any oral or written statements to the contrary are hereby expressly disavowed and should not be relied upon by any prospective employee.

New Hire Agreement:

Either the employer or employee may terminate this Employment Agreement at any time or for any reason by providing 2 weeks of notice (10 working days). It is agreed that the employer will not provide 2 weeks of notice in the case of an employee who is terminated because of misconduct.

In Employee Handbook:

Your employment is for no definite period and can be terminated with or without cause at any time by you or the company. No employee in this company has the authority to make agreements with you concerning the length of your employment.

---

2. To avoid union organization;
3. To avoid litigation and liability arising from allegations of violations of the civil rights laws, wrongful discharge, or torts committed in connection with employment termination; and
4. To stimulate current employees to stay and employees of other employers to come."

Termination Policy

A termination policy normally covers the following topics.

- Notice requirement
- Discharges
- Final paycheck
- Severance pay
- Benefits
- References
- Clearance procedures

Your policy should state exactly how much *notice* you require of your employees. Two weeks is normal for hourly employees, and up to 4 weeks for management employees. You should also state the negative consequences for the failure of an employee to give adequate notice, such as how it could affect payment for accrued vacation time, references, and eligibility for rehire.

Your statement of notice is also important when firing employees. If you require employees to give you 2 weeks' notice, you must also give 2 weeks' notice, or pay in lieu of giving notice, to fired employees. This rule does not apply to employees discharged for gross misconduct, which requires immediate dismissal, or to new employees on probation, as this relationship can typically be terminated by either party at any time without notice.

For *discharges*, you need to develop a statement naming who has the authority to fire an employee and the procedure for doing so. It is a good idea to forbid on-the-spot firing and take the safer route of suspending the employee pending an investigation, as in the following steps.

1. The highest ranking manager present will suspend the employee without pay immediately, pending an investigation. It should be explained to the employee that if the investigation shows that the suspension was not warranted, the employee will be entitled to be paid for the suspension days.

2. An investigation should be made and all facts documented. If there is a human resource department, it should be notified.
3. If firing the employee is justified, have the employee's final paycheck prepared so it can be given to the employee during the termination interview.
4. Arrange for the employee to return for a meeting and prepare the Termination Interview Checklist (Fig. 5-5, discussed later in this chapter).
5. The general manager, department head, or human resources department representative should attend the termination interview and make sure all paperwork has been prepared correctly.

Your discharge policy should also cover other forms of discharge, such as layoffs.

In most states you are required to have the employee's *final paycheck* ready at the termination interview or within a certain number of hours. The final paycheck may include *severance pay*, extra pay given to an employee at the time of termination.

Severance pay is, in most cases, based on the number of years of the employee's service, and the employee must have completed between 6 months to 1 year of service to qualify. A common formula used to determine severance pay for hourly employees is 1/2 to 1 week of pay for each year of service up to a specific limit, such as 26 weeks. Whatever your policy is, it should be clearly spelled out and consistently followed. In the statement of your policy, be sure to include who is eligible for severance pay, how it is calculated, how it is paid (lump sum or continuing payroll checks), and whether the company has the right to change or cancel the plan at any time. Figure 5-2 shows a sample severance pay policy statement for hourly employees.

There are many federal and state regulations concerning the terminated employee's rights to certain *benefits*. In addition to these regulations, employers are often guided by the following considerations.

- The use of benefits to attract and retain employees more than to assist terminated employees
- The reason that the employee is leaving
- The employee's length of service
- The employee's grade level

A brief description of some of the more important laws follows.

The 1986 Consolidated Omnibus Budget Reconciliation Act (COBRA) requires that employers provide their employees, spouses, and dependent children the chance to continue their health insurance

Fig. 5-2 **SAMPLE SEVERANCE PAY POLICY FOR HOURLY EMPLOYEES**

Human Resources Policy and Procedure

Subject: Severance pay for nonexempt employees

Policy: It is our intention to provide nonexempt full-time employees with severance pay benefits in circumstances where there was no misconduct on the part of the employee. The purpose of severance pay is to help the employee's transition to a new job or retirement.

Procedure: 1. If a full-time employee is terminated for any of the following reasons, he or she is eligible for severance pay benefits as described in 2.

- Unsatisfactory work performance
- Encouraged early retirement
- Layoff
- Job elimination

             2. The severance pay allowance is as follows:

- Two and one-half days of pay for each full year of service
- The maximum allowance is 13 weeks

             3. Severance pay is paid in a lump sum in the final paycheck.

The company has the right to change or cancel this severance pay policy and procedure at any time.

under the employer's plan at group rates. Monthly premiums plus a 2 percent administrative fee can be paid for up to 18 months. A spouse or dependent child may decide to purchase coverage even if the former employee declines. The coverage must be identical to that provided for employed plan participants. All employers with 20 or more employees must comply with COBRA. An employer is not obligated to offer this continuation of benefits to employees terminated for gross misconduct. Figure 5-3 is an example of a letter informing an employee of his or her rights to continued coverage.

Several laws provide guaranteed pension benefits for terminated employees, including the Employee Retirement Income Security Act (ERISA) of 1974, as amended by the Retirement Equity Act (REA) of 1984 and the Tax Reform Act (TRA) of 1986. If a terminated employee worked for the period of time needed for "vesting" in a qualified plan, he or she has the right to the benefit at retirement age. To be vested means that the employee has the right to receive a portion or all of his or her retirement benefits at retirement age despite termination of employment before his or her reaching retirement age.

There are both federal and state laws regarding payment for vacation time. You are generally expected to pay a terminated employee for any earned vacation time that was not used.

It is not a good idea to issue *letters of reference* to employees who are being terminated for misconduct or poor performance. Although you may want to help an individual to find other employment, a letter of reference implying a satisfactory rating may wind up in court as evidence that the employee was doing an adequate job. Likewise, it is not a good idea to furnish an employee with a letter explaining the reasons for dismissal, unless required by state law, as you run the risk of litigation for defamation of character. To be safe, such references should be limited to dates of employment, final position title, final work location, and final wage.

Clearance procedures typically include having the employee hand in uniforms, ID card, keys, name tag, and any other items issued to him or her. Sometimes an employee is asked to fill out a separation form (Fig. 5-4) that lists the official reason for termination and other administrative information.

Alternatives to Dismissal

There are several alternatives to dismissal. These include transfer, demotion, and dehiring. In some cases, an employee may be better suited to transfer to a different position with new job duties that suit

Fig. 5-3   SAMPLE COBRA LETTER

Date:

Employee Name:

Social Security Number:

Date of Termination:

Election Expiration Date:

Dear Employee,

Federal law requires us to extend the opportunity for you to extend temporarily the coverage of your group health insurance plan at your own cost as follows:

1. This coverage applies to you, as well as your spouse and dependents, provided they were previously covered. You may purchase either single or family coverage as appropriate.
2. The terms of the policy will be identical to that provided to you previously.
3. You can continue to pay for this coverage for up to 18 months. Under certain circumstances, you may be eligible for up to 36 months.
4. The cost for such coverage is at our group rates plus a 2 percent administrative fee. Premiums are due monthly. Your current monthly premiums are as follows: _____.

If you wish to continue your group health coverage, complete the attached enrollment form and return it to this office in the envelope provided before the expiration date noted above. If you do not, you will not receive another offer to do so.

Sincerely,

enc.

Director of Human
Resources

Fig. 5-4 SAMPLE SEPARATION FORM

SEPARATION FORM

Employee Name _____

Employee Position _____ Department _____

Last Date of Employment _____

I am leaving my position because: _____

_____

_____

_____

_____

1. I understand that I must clean out my locker and turn in my name tag, uniforms, and keys before I can receive my final paycheck.
2. I have reported all work-related injuries.
3. I understand that my benefits terminate as of my last date of employment and that I must notify you within 60 days if I want to continue health benefits at my own expense. My rights to the pension plan have been explained to me.
4. I am entitled to receive the following termination pay:

   Unused vacation allowance _____ Workdays

   _____ _____ Workdays

5. My final paycheck will be ready _____. (Please note below your address if you would like it mailed to you.)

| Number and Street | City | State | Zip Code |

Employee's Signature   Date

Human Resource Representative Signature   Date

him or her better. However, an ineffective or disruptive employee in one department quite often turns out to be just as ineffective or disruptive in another department.

Another possibility is demotion, that is, placing the employee in a lower-ranking job. In some cases, this is a viable solution for an employee who is having a hard time performing up to standards but who you feel could do less demanding work effectively. Unfortunately, demotion often does not work when both rank and pay are lowered. About 70 percent of employees so demoted will quit. If you think an employee can handle a demotion in rank, you may consider keeping the rate of pay the same.

Dehiring employees means encouraging them to quit by giving them meaningless duties to perform. Their jobs are often reduced to busywork in the hope that they will become totally bored and disgusted and leave. About 70 percent of dehired employees eventually quit; however, your worst employees will not. They stay forever, or so it seems, so dehiring is rarely an answer for this group.

Should This Employee Be Discharged?

The decision to discharge an employee is a very serious one, as it impacts heavily on your employee, and on you if the employee eventually sues for wrongful discharge. Your human resources department representative should always be contacted and consulted prior to your dismissing anyone. Your first consideration in deciding whether or not to discharge an employee is to make sure such action is not prohibited by federal law, as shown in the following list (Granholm, 1991).*

- Discharging an employee on the basis of race, color, sex, or national origin (Title VII of the Civil Rights Act of 1964)
- Discharging in retaliation for filing discrimination charges (Title VII of the Civil Rights Act of 1964)
- Discharging an employee for testifying against company at Equal Employment Opportunity Commission hearings (Title VII of the Civil Rights Act of 1964)
- Discharging an employee for helping other employees who have been discriminated against by the company to exercise their legal rights (Title VII of the Civil Rights Act of 1964)

* Adapted from: *Handbook of Employee Termination*, Axel R. Granholm. Copyright © 1991 by John Wiley & Sons, Inc. Reprinted by permission.

- Discharging an older employee, 40 years of age or more, because of age (The Age Discrimination in Employment Act of 1967, as amended)
- Forcing retirement or permanent layoff of an older employee (The Age Discrimination in Employment Act of 1967, as amended)
- Discharging an older employee in a permanent layoff using standards that are not applied universally to all affected employees (The Age Discrimination in Employment Act of 1967, as amended)
- Discharging an employee because she is pregnant (The Pregnancy Discrimination Act of 1978)
- Discharging an employee in retaliation for filing an OSHA complaint (The Occupational Safety and Health Act of 1970)
- Discharging an employee in retaliation for requesting a state or federal inspection of unsafe working conditions (The Occupational Safety and Health Act of 1970)
- Discharging an employee in retaliation for testifying against the company in an OHSA-related court action (The Occupational Safety and Health Act of 1970)
- Discharging a handicapped employee because of the handicap (Americans with Disabilities Act of 1990)
- Discharging a Vietnam-era veteran during his or her first year of reemployment without "good cause" (The Vietnam-Era Veterans' Readjustment Assistance Act of 1974)
- Discharging an employee to avoid paying pension or benefit plan such as group health insurance plans (The Employee Retirement Income Security Act of 1974)
- Discharging an employee because of his or her obligation to perform jury service
- Discharging for performing duties as a member of the National Guard
- Discharging in retaliation for refusal to perform an illegal act on behalf of the employer
- Discharging in retaliation for whistle-blowing concerning the illegal acts of the employer, such as making false statements
- Discharging an employee who is exercising a legal right, such as filing for workers' compensation
- Discharging for participation in union activities or union-organizing efforts
- Discharging in retaliation for helping the government prepare or prosecute a case against the employer

Once you are sure the discharge does not fit into any of the above categories and the discipline or corrective action policy has been appropriately followed, see if you can answer yes to each of the following questions.

Did the employee know the rule and was he or she warned about the consequences of violating the rule? Are these understandings confirmed and acknowledged in writing? Prior knowledge of a rule is not an issue in the case of gross misconduct, such as theft, in which the employee is expected to know that such conduct will result in his or her termination.

Were management's expectations of the employee reasonable? Was the rule reasonable? Management, of course, cannot ask an employee to do anything that might be unsafe, illegal, dishonest, or indecent.

Did management make a reasonable effort to help the employee resolve the problem before termination, and is there proof of such? Is there thorough and accurate documentation of all prior counselings, warnings, suspensions, and performance evaluations?

Was a final warning given to the employee explaining that discharge would result from another rule violation or unsatisfactory performance? Was this final warning in writing, and did the employee sign it to acknowledge understanding of its terms and conditions?

In the case of misconduct, did the employee act in willful and deliberate disregard of reasonable employer expectations? Was the situation within his or her control? If the situation was beyond the employee's personal control, he or she cannot be charged with misconduct. For example, perhaps the employee did not know about a change in procedures because he or she was off the day this was discussed at a meeting; perhaps the employee did not have the right equipment to do the job; perhaps the error was just an accident or the result of inexperience. In each of these instances, the employee's action was beyond personal control and cannot be grounds for termination.

Was management's investigation of the final offense conducted fairly and objectively, and did it involve someone other than the employee's direct supervisor? If there is a human resources department, was it appropriately contacted and involved? It is best that the employee's supervisor not function alone, filling the roles of accuser, judge, and jury. Is there substantial proof that the employee is guilty?

Is dismissal of the employee in line with the employee's prior work record and length of service? When an employee has many years of service that are documented as satisfactory or better, he or she is generally entitled to more time to improve before being dismissed.

Did the employee have an opportunity to hear the facts and respond to them within a nonthreatening environment? Was the employee able to bring another person into the disciplinary interview if so requested?

Has this employee been treated as others in similar circumstances? Has this rule been consistently enforced in the past? If the rule has not been consistently enforced in the past, you may have to forgo termination of the employee and instead go back a step, such as to suspension. When you begin to enforce again a rule that has not been enforced for some time, you must inform employees prior to the change.

Is the action nondiscriminatory? Has equal treatment been given to members of protected groups (minorities, women, employees over 40 years of age) and nonprotected groups?

These questions are only guidelines for determining whether there is just cause to terminate an employee. Even if you can answer yes to every question presented here, there is still no guarantee that you will not end up in court. The laws vary from state to state and year to year. In addition, presenting your case at an unemployment hearing is quite different from presenting it before the Equal Employment Opportunity Commission.

The Termination Interview

There are not many people who really enjoy telling an employee that he or she is terminated, fired, or dismissed. The best way to reduce your nervousness and make it less stressful for the employee is to prepare for the termination interview by using the Termination Interview Checklist (Fig. 5-5). This sheet can help you to do the following:

Select a good time and place to conduct the interview.

Determine who will be present at the meeting (you should have at least one person as a witness), as well as whether the employee needs to be escorted out of the building

Develop your opening statement and practice it

Determine how best to respond to possible employee reactions

Determine the final pay, severance pay, and benefits to which the employee is entitled

Develop a list of clearance procedures to be performed at the end of the interview

The timing and place for the interview are important. Although conventional wisdom says to fire an employee at the end of a work-week, that is not necessarily the best time. By firing the employee at the beginning of the workweek, you give him or her a chance to start immediately looking for a new job, instead of complaining and becoming upset at home. Nor is it wise to terminate employees near major events such as holidays, birthdays, or dates of anniversary with the company. Try to arrange a time when the employee can clean out his or her locker without other employees present. The meeting should take place in a private room so that, should the employee become unruly, guests and co-workers will not be disturbed. A room in the human resources department is ideal.

Now that you have prepared for the interview, it is time to speak with the employee. Although you may be nervous, it is probable that the employee is nervous as well. In many cases, the employee knows that he or she is likely to be fired, and is anxious to get it over with too. Employees who are fired are often relieved and go on to find new jobs that are much more satisfying. In some cases, you might even feel that you did the employee a favor. Following are the steps for a termination interview. Be sure you use your Termination Interview Checklist (Fig. 5-5) as a guide.

1. Do not beat around the bush. Avoid small talk and tell the employee that he or she is being dismissed and why. Do so in a firm, calm, and objective manner. Avoid a discussion of all the details leading up to this decision. This is not the time for that; there have surely been plenty of previous counselings. Instead, state the category under which the discipline problem falls, such as excessive absenteeism, and mention the last step taken and how it was made clear that the employee faced termination for one more offense. Clearly communicate that the decision has been made and that there is no possibility for negotiation. Explain that the decision is a joint decision in which others, such as the general manager and human resources manager, have been involved. Reinforced in this manner, your authority will not be questioned as readily.
2. At this point, listen to and accept the responses of the employee. Be prepared for any type of response, such as anger, tears,

Fig. 5-5   SAMPLE TERMINATION INTERVIEW CHECKLIST

TERMINATION INTERVIEW CHECKLIST

Employee Name: _____

Employee Position: _____ Department: _____

Employment Date: _____ Termination Date: _____

1. **Decide on where the interview will take place and when.**

   (Avoid firing at end of workweek or near the time of major events such as
   birthdays and holidays. Choose a time when the employee can clear out
   his or her belongings without other employees present. Select a quiet
   place where you will not be interrupted and the employee will not disturb
   others upon leaving.)

   _____

   _____

   _____

   _____

2. **Determine who will be present at the meeting and whether the employee
   needs an escort out of the building.**

   (There should be at least one person as a witness, and probably a
   representative from human resources present as well. If the employee is
   a member of a bargaining unit, use the contract as your guide.)

   _____

   _____

   _____

3. **Develop an opening statement and practice it.**

   (Write out exactly what you are going to tell the employee. Make sure
   you state clearly that the employee is being terminated and include a
   brief summary of the reason(s). Make it clear to the employee that there
   are no options.)

   _____

   _____

   _____

   _____

4. **Determine how best to respond to possible employee reactions.**

   (Think about how you expect the employee to respond and how you can
   handle each type of response. Your goal during the interview is to let the
   employee respond to the termination, within limits, and then proceed
   with getting the necessary information across.)

   Possible Reactions: _____

   _____

Fig. 5-5 Continued

Your Responses: _____

_____

Record below any threats the employee makes about legal action during the interview.

_____

_____

_____

5. **Determine the final pay, severance pay, and benefits to which the employee is entitled, and communicate them.**

Pay:

_____ Pay in lieu of notice   _____ Workdays
(only in the case of unsatisfactory
work performance)

_____ Accrued vacation   _____ Workdays

Payment by: _____ Lump sum _____ Payroll checks

Benefits:
Entitled to: Explained:

_____   _____ Group health insurance continuation

_____   _____ Vested rights in pension plan

OTHER: _____

6. **Clearance procedures**

Make sure employee hands in the following:

_____ Locker keys

_____ Uniforms

_____ Name tag

_____ ID card

Completed by: Date:

_____   _____

Table 5-1   How to React to Employees' Emotional Responses

Type of Emotional Response	What You Can Do
1. Crying	▪ Let the employee cry it out. ▪ Do not apologize for your actions. ▪ Show concern by offering a tissue, something to drink, or a moment of privacy if appropriate. ▪ Stay calm and businesslike, think about the next step in the interview.
2. Shouting and Cursing	▪ Keep your own emotions under control and maintain a calm and cool demeanor. ▪ Make it perfectly clear to the employee that you will continue the conversation only when the shouting stops. Use your normal tone of voice; do not show irritation. ▪ Tell the employee you would like him or her to know the arrangement for termination pay and benefits.
3. Unresponsive	▪ Be empathetic, but also continue the interview. ▪ Do not ask the employee questions such as "How could you be shocked at this news?" Do not play counselor when the employee withdraws. ▪ Confirm all details in a letter.
4. Employee leaves after your opening statement	▪ Tell employee that you really do not want him or her to miss hearing the arrangements made for termination pay and benefits.

amazement, or hostility. Table 5-1 describes how to react to four different types of responses.

3. Now is the time to say something positive to the employee to maintain his or her self-esteem, which at this point is probably sagging. Make a statement about something you, and as well as others, really like about the employee. Perhaps the employee has a good sense of humor or performed a certain aspect of his or her job very well.

4. Move on next to a discussion of final pay, severance pay, and benefits to which the employee is entitled.
5. Finally, explain your clearance procedures and give the employee clear instructions about what to do after your discussion. Do you want the employee to go straight to his or her locker, clean it out, and leave quietly? Is there someone who will escort the employee out of the building? This is advisable if the employee is being dismissed because of gross misconduct.
6. End the interview by standing up and moving toward the door. Try to close on a positive, friendly note.

After the interview, be sure to document important details, including the employee's reaction, any threats that may have been made, and any comments made about the fairness of the decision. Be sure to keep everything confidential; inform only those individuals who must know. If you tell the employee's former co-workers about the dismissal, you are leaving yourself open to being sued for slander.

General Guidelines for Conducting a Termination Interview

- Avoid making any physical gesture, such as shaking hands or putting your hand on the employee's shoulder, which could be taken the wrong way by someone who is upset and angry.
- Maintain a calm, businesslike manner throughout the entire interview. Any inappropriate remarks on your part could be used by the employee to justify (in court) that he or she was traumatized by the termination interview.
- Be understanding and helpful.
- Be very careful not to say anything that might provoke employee hostility or encourage rebuttals.
- Speak simply and directly.
- Keep the pace moving. The entire interview should be over in about 10 to 20 minutes.

6

Special Concerns: Substance Abuse, Attendance Problems, and Sexual Harassment

Substance Abuse

Substance abuse is found in the workplace as it is elsewhere. The extent of alcohol abuse is much greater than that of all illegal drugs combined. Illegal drugs include cocaine, crack, heroin, hallucinogens such as LSD and PCP, mescaline, marijuana, amphetamines (speed), barbituates (downers), and codeine. The costs of substance abuse in the workplace, which has been going on for a long time, are very high. There are some interesting statistics on substance abuse (Thompson, 1990).

- Between 10 to 23 percent of all American workers use dangerous drugs on the job.
- As many as one in five American workers has a drug and/or alcohol problem.
- Over half of young workers entering the work force have used illegal drugs.
- The Bureau of Labor Statistics reports that 18.8 percent of employees, and 24.4 percent of applicants, in the retail trade tested positive for drugs.
- The National Institute on Drug Abuse estimates that one out of five employees from 18 to 25 years of age, and one of eight from 26 to 34 years of age, uses drugs on the job.
- Employees who have a problem with alcohol abuse
  Are absent two times more often than other employees
  Have two to three times more accidents
  Collect three times more sickness and accident benefits

- Employees who have a problem with drug abuse
  Are late for work three times more often than other employees
  Have over two times more absences of 8 days or more
  Use three times the normal level of sick benefits
  Are five times more likely to file workers' compensation claims
  Are involved in accidents over three times more often
- Drug and alcohol abuse cause lost productivity, absenteeism, and medical expenses, which cost employers an average of 3 percent of their total payroll.

When considering substance abuse, it is important to understand the difference between substance abuse and addiction. Between 10 and 20 percent of individuals who abuse alcohol or drugs will actually become addicted. The abuser consciously desires to abuse a substance, the addicted person has to.

Based on the facts that substance abuse in the workplace has become a tremendous concern and that it can be dealt with effectively, there have been numerous government initiatives to deal with it. Of particular interest is the Drug Free Workplace Act of 1988, which requires most federal contractors and anyone who receives federal grants to provide a drug-free workplace by doing the following:

Informing employees that they are prohibited from engaging in any of the following in the workplace: unlawful manufacture, distribution, dispensation, possession, or use of a controlled substance; informing employees what actions they can expect if they violate this prohibition (this policy must be in writing)

Giving employees a copy of the policy and asking them to abide by it as a condition of continued employment

Informing employees of the dangers of drug abuse at work, and telling them about any available counseling, rehabilitation, and employee assistance programs

Making a good-faith effort to maintain a drug-free workplace

These represent some of the major requirements for employers.

If you are not covered by this law, what can you as an employer do to fight substance abuse in the workplace? In 1989 President Bush submitted the administration's 1989 National Drug Control Strategy and encouraged employers to do the following:

Develop and communicate to all employees a clear drug policy, setting out expectations of behavior, employee rights and responsibilities, and actions to be taken in response to an employee's use of illegal drugs

Establish an employee assistance program or other appropriate
   mechanism
Train supervisors in how to identify and deal with employees who
   are using drugs
Educate employees about the established plan
Provide careful means to identify employees who use drugs, including drug testing where appropriate

A discussion of each of these points follows in turn.

SUBSTANCE ABUSE POLICY AND PROCEDURE

To prevent substance abuse in the workplace, you need first to
develop your own clearly written policy and procedures. Figure 6-1 is
a sample policy and procedures statement. Your policy should explain
management's position on substance abuse. Some issues you might
address in your policy include (Thompson, 1990)

Your concern for employee health and safety
Recognition of the dangers that substance abuse presents in the
   workplace
Your position on illegal drug possession and drug-related activities
Your position on alcohol consumption in the workplace and off
   premises that affects job performance
Your position when substance abuse affects job performance
When drug testing will be used
Availability of employee assistance or other programs
Penalties for violating policies
Education programs available
Individuals covered by the policy

In general, employers are concerned about substance abuse only to
the extent that it interferes with job performance and employee
health and safety. In these situations, the employee is disciplined
according to the discipline policy and may be referred to an employee
assistance or other program. If the employee continues to have problems and is about to be terminated, you need to offer, one last time, an
opportunity to get help. If the employee agrees, he or she will not be
terminated. If the employee disagrees, termination action is taken.
Written procedures are essential to the success of your program.
Well-written procedures are specific, simple, understandable, and not
too hard to comply with. Following are some of the subjects that
should be included in the statement of your procedures.

Fig. 6-1   SAMPLE SUBSTANCE ABUSE POLICY AND PROCEDURES STATEMENT

PERSONNEL POLICIES AND PROCEDURES

DISTRIBUTION: ALL ADMINISTRATIVE   SUBJECT: SUBSTANCE ABUSE POLICY
MANAGERIAL/SUPERVISORY
STAFF

EFFECTIVE DATE: 3/1/91

REVISION DATE: 2/15/92

All revisions are marked by an asterisk (*)

I. General Policy

The Keefer Company is committed to programs that promote safety in the workplace, employee health, and well-being, and that promote a positive image of the institution in the community. Consistent with the spirit and intent of this commitment, the Keefer Company has developed this policy statement regarding the sale, use, possession, and distribution of drugs and alcohol by all company employees and agents.

Employee involvement with drugs and alcohol can adversely affect job performance and employee morale, jeopardize employee and guest safety, and undermine the public's confidence. Such involvement is particularly unacceptable in an industry like ours in light of the nature of our role in society and the potentially disastrous consequences to guests that may result from an employee's impaired condition. Our goal, and the purpose of this policy, therefore, is to establish and maintain a safe workplace and a healthy and efficient work force free from the effects of drug and alcohol abuse, and to extend to employees having an addictive disease an opportunity for effective treatment and rehabilitation.

II. Employee Assistance Program

The Keefer Company encourages any employee with a drug or alcohol problem to contact the EAP, the Human Resources Department, or any recognized external evaluation, referral, or treatment agency for assistance. The company subscribes to the premise that addictive diseases are entitled to the same consideration and offer of treatment that is extended to any other disease. All communications and records will be maintained on a confidential basis.[1] Employees will not be subject to discipline for voluntarily acknowledging their drug/alcohol problems, nor will job security or promotional opportunities be jeopardized as a consequence only of having an addictive disease, except to the extent that the manifestations of the disease interfere with the employee's performance of his or her job. However, this will *not* excuse violations of the Substance Abuse Policy, for which the employee is subject to

---

[1] There may be limited exceptions to this guarantee in instances (1) where there may be a clear and present danger presented to the welfare of the employee or another person; (2) where records or testimony might be subject to subpoena or other legal process; or (3) where the employee consents to disclosure.

Fig. 6-1 Continued

discipline. Employees who utilize the company's Employee Assistance Program or any other treatment resource will be expected to meet existing job performance standards and established work rules within the framework of established administrative practices. A request for assistance does not exempt the employee from routine performance expectations, nor does it confer any immunity, legal or disciplinary, from the consequences of misconduct.

III. Rules Regarding Drugs and Alcohol

Whenever the capacity of an employee to function on the job has been diminished to the point where guests' safety may be compromised, supervisory personnel will have the responsibility for taking immediate action to: (a) remove the impaired employee from guest contact; (b) initiate standard fitness for duty guidelines and/or disciplinary procedures; and (c) refer the individual to the Employee Assistance Program. The justification for taking such actions shall be observable unsatisfactory job performance or behavior. For further information, please refer to the Fitness for Duty guidelines.

A. Use, Possession, Transportation, Sale, and Distribution

The use, possession, sale, or distribution of drugs or alcohol by employees while on company property or company business shall be cause for immediate discharge. Illegal substances will be confiscated, and the appropriate law enforcement agencies may be notified.

B. Drugs/Alcohol in System

1. Alcohol

An employee found to have a blood-alcohol concentration of .05% or more (or its equivalent as determined by a different diagnostic test such as a Breathalyzer) while on company property or on company business shall receive a 5-day suspension on the first offense and shall be required to participate in the Employee Assistance Program. In addition, the employee shall be subject to random drug and alcohol testing. If the employee refuses to participate in the EAP and the terms of a chemical dependency treatment agreement and/or violates any rules set forth in this policy at any time thereafter, he or she shall be subject to immediate discharge.

2. Marijuana/Hashish

An employee found to have detectable concentrations of marijuana (or its metabolites) in his or her system shall receive a 5-day suspension on the first offense and shall be required to participate in the Employee Assistance Program. In addition, the employee shall be subject to random drug and alcohol testing. If the employee refuses to participate in the EAP and the terms of a chemical dependency treatment agreement and/or violates any rules set forth in this policy at any time thereafter, he or she shall be subject to immediate discharge.

Fig. 6-1 Continued

---

3. Drugs Other Than Marijuana or Alcohol

An employee found to have detectable concentrations of any drug other than marijuana or alcohol in his or her system, including, but not limited to, heroin, cocaine, morphine, phencyclidine (PCP), amphetamines, barbiturates, or hallucinogens (or metabolites of any such drugs), shall receive a 5-day suspension on the first offense and shall be required to participate in the Employee Assistance Program. In addition, the employee shall be subject to random drug and alcohol testing. If the employee refuses to participate in the EAP and the terms of a chemical dependency treatment agreement and/or violates any rules set forth in this policy at any time thereafter, he or she shall be subject to immediate discharge.

4. Testing for Drugs/Alcohol in System

An employee may be required to submit to blood, urine, or other diagnostic tests to detect alcohol and/or drugs (or drug metabolites) in his or her system whenever the employee is involved in an on-the-job accident or the employee's observed behavior raises a reasonable suspicion of drug or alcohol use. (A bargaining unit employee is entitled to have a union representative present, if immediately available, during the initial collecting of a specimen.) If an initial screening test indicates positive findings, a confirmatory test will be conducted.

Employees with a prior violation of the Drug and Alcohol Policy will be subject to random testing.

Any employee who refuses to submit to testing shall be subject to disciplinary action up to and including discharge.

C. Other Rules and Provisions

1. Searches

The Keefer Company reserves the right to carry out reasonable searches of employees and their property, including, but not limited to, lockers, lunch boxes, and private vehicles, if parked on company property. (A bargaining unit employee whose person or property is to be searched is entitled to have a union representative present, if immediately available, while the search is being conducted.) An employee who refuses to submit immediately to such a search shall be subject to disciplinary action up to and including discharge.

2. Drug Paraphernalia

Employees are prohibited from bringing drug paraphernalia onto company property at any time. An employee who possesses or distributes such paraphernalia while on company property shall be subject to disciplinary action, up to and including discharge.

3. Off-Duty Arrests/Convictions

An employee who is arrested for, or convicted of, a drug offense that involves the off-duty sale, distribution, or possession of illegal drugs must promptly inform the company of the arrest, the nature of the charges, and the ultimate disposition of the charges. Failure to do so constitutes grounds for discipline, up to and including

Fig. 6-1 Continued

discharge. Such arrest/conviction may subject the employee to discipline, up to and including discharge, depending on the circumstances.

 4. Over-the-Counter or Prescribed Medications

Over-the-counter or prescription medications may have pharmacological effects that can impair job functioning and performance. Additionally, many such medications may be abused, even if obtained through legal means, by exceeding the customary dosage. Employees taking such medications are responsible for using such drugs in an appropriate manner, becoming aware of the potential side effects of any such drug, and informing their supervisor of their use of medications which might potentially impair their job performance. Employees who intentionally abuse medications such as (but not limited to) tranquilizers, sedative-hypnotics, analgesics, antidepressants, or diet pills shall be subjected to the same disciplinary sanctions prescribed for illicit drugs in this policy (i.e., a 5-day suspension, random testing, and referral to the EAP). Employees whose impairment can be demonstrated to be the result of an inadvertent, unpredictable, or typical reaction to an over-the-counter or prescription medication shall be absolved of any responsibility for such an incident.

 5. Reporting Violations of the Drug and Alcohol Policy

It is each employee's responsibility to report immediately any unsafe working conditions or hazardous activities that may jeopardize his or her safety or the safety of fellow employees, guests, or visitors. This responsibility includes the immediate reporting of any violation of the Substance Abuse Policy. An employee who fails to report such a violation may be subject to disciplinary action, up to and including discharge.

 6. Job Applicants

Applicants for employment with the Keefer Company may be given blood, urine, or other diagnostic tests to detect alcohol and/or drugs (or drug metabolites) in their systems. Successful completion of the test is a condition of employment.

 7. Reemployment

Any individual who leaves the company through layoff, resignation, or termination for a period exceeding 90 days will be required to submit to blood, urine, or other diagnostic tests to detect alcohol and/or drugs (or drug metabolites) in their systems prior to reentry into the work force. Positive test results for alcohol or drugs will be considered in deciding whether the employee shall be permitted to return to work.

 8. Progressive Discipline Not Applicable

The disciplinary steps set forth in the Employee Handbook providing for progressive discipline (e.g., first written warning, second written warning, probation, discharge) or the three-step process for Level II Infractions *do not apply* to violations of the Substance Abuse Policy. The discipline to be imposed for violations of the Substance Abuse Policy shall be governed solely by the provisions set forth herein.

Source: Adapted from Jersey Shore Medical Center Personnel Policies and Procedures, Neptune, NJ. Reprinted with permission.

A DEFINITION OF SUBSTANCE ABUSE

Substance abuse is usually defined as working under the influence of, using, or being impaired by alcohol or any drug, where job performance or safety of employees is adversely affected. Drugs include both illegal and some legal drugs, such as prescription or over-the-counter medications that adversely affect job performance.

NOTICE AND EMPLOYEE ACKNOWLEDGMENT

You can give employees notice of your policy in many ways: handing out copies to new and current employees, posting the policy on a bulletin board, conducting a training session, explaining the policy in company publications such as a newsletter, mailing letters to the employees' homes, and/or putting notices into paycheck envelopes.

DRUG TESTING OF APPLICANTS AND EMPLOYEES

Drug testing is probably the best way to reduce drug abuse in the workplace. It sends a clear message that drug use will not be tolerated and provides a deterrent that is better than education. Drug testing of applicants is widely accepted and implemented and is probably the most extensively used program for drug testing. An increasing number of companies, including more Fortune 500 companies, are performing drug tests on applicants (Thompson, 1990). Employers who do this inform applicants of their substance abuse policy, including the fact that employment is denied if the results of the test are positive. There are many types of testing, including across-the-board testing, annual physical or fitness for duty testing, probationary employee testing, postaccident testing, and "for-cause" testing. Most programs include "for-cause" testing, which means that if the employer has a reasonable suspicion that an employee may be impaired as a result of substance abuse, the employee will be asked to take a drug test. Examples of causes include repeated failure to follow instructions or violation of safety procedures. Testing should be based on specific incidents of job performance problems, and the tested employee should be asked to sign a consent form.

VOLUNTARY REFERRAL

In this procedure, employees are encouraged to use employee assistance program (EAP) services or to enter a rehabilitation program before referral to drug testing or to the EAP becomes mandatory.

REHABILITATION OPTIONS

To employees whose results of drug-testing are positive, employers frequently give two options: referral to the EAP or, directly, to rehabilitation. In this section of your statement, you can explain your procedures for dealing with rehabilitation options, time off for counseling, and time off and benefits while an employee is in a full-time rehabilitation program.

POSTREHABILITATION AGREEMENTS

This section explains your policy regarding the return of the employee to his or her job. It often describes a "last chance agreement," by which the employee agrees to stay free of proscribed substances in order to return to work and keep his or her job. Usually, termination results if the employee tests positive during a certain period of time or leaves rehabilitation.

EMPLOYEE FAILURE TO COOPERATE

You should spell out very clearly what will happen to employees who fail to cooperate with any aspect of the substance abuse program, such as those who refuse to agree to a drug test or to seek rehabilitation as a condition of employment. Employees are commonly terminated for not cooperating.

Because the laws concerning this topic are complex and increasing, be sure to have legal counsel review your policy and procedure prior to implementation.

EMPLOYEE ASSISTANCE PROGRAMS

Those counseling programs called employee assistance programs (EAPs) are an expansion of traditional occupational alcoholism programs, which began to appear 40 years ago. About one-third of the U.S. work force has access to EAPs, according to the Association of Labor-Management Administrators and Consultants on Alcoholism, based in Arlington, Virginia, which represents about 6,000 member EAP practitioners. Larger companies are more likely to have EAPs than smaller companies. Companies such as Marriott, Kentucky Fried Chicken, and Lettuce Entertain You offer counseling and referral services to some or all of their employees.

EAPs function to help troubled employees in personal crises, as well as those with emotional, alcohol, or drug abuse problems. In a time when the foodservice industry needs to retain employees, EAPs can help to get employees back on their feet and back to work. The six most common functions of an EAP are as follows.

1. To identify employees who need help
2. To educate and train supervisors and employees about what the EAP counselor does and how to refer employees to him or her
3. To motivate employees who need help to seek and accept help

4. To assess the employee's problem in order to direct him or her to an appropriate source of help, such as Alcoholics Anonymous
5. To assist employees in getting the services they need (such as rehabilitation)
6. To help employees who have received assistance to prevent relapses

An operator may hire its own counselor to administer the program, use an outside counselor under contract to the EAP, or use a counselor affiliated with a nonprofit social services group. Outside companies estimate that EAPs cost the employer from $.75 to $3.00 per employee per month. The price varies according to the number of services provided. Although the scope of services varies from company to company, most include initial consultation to determine the nature and extent of the problem and counseling targeted at easing or resolving this problem.

When starting an EAP, a company should have a policy statement written to explain its objectives for the program. This statement should include the fact that the EAP is strictly confidential. This information, including how to use the program, should be explained clearly to employees. In addition, managers and supervisors need to be trained as to how and when to make referrals; if an employee is having personal problems that are affecting job performance, the EAP program should be suggested as a source of help. Referrals are also appropriate if an employee appears to be angry, confused, depressed, or withdrawn.

When referring an employee to the program, follow this list of do's and don'ts.

- Do emphasize confidentiality
- Do explain that going for help does not exempt the employee from disciplinary procedures nor does it include special privileges.
- Do stick to discussing job performance and explain in very specific terms what the employee needs to do in order to perform up to expectations.
- Do give the employee the appropriate information in writing on how to contact an EAP counselor.
- Don't try to diagnose the employee's problem, nor ask why the employee is performing in a certain way. This only leads to excuse making.
- Don't go into depth with the employee about personal problems. Don't become the employee's counselor.
- Don't take responsibility for solving the employee's problems.

- Don't be swayed by emotional pleas, sympathy tactics, or hard luck stories.

Successful EAP programs share the following characteristics:

The program is accessible 24 hours a day, 7 days a week.
The employees are given the phone number of the EAP office.
The program is carried out by qualified professionals who are understanding of personal problems.
Involvement of the employee's family is encouraged in situations where it is relevant to treatment.
The program should be advertised, and available, to the entire family.
Confidentiality must be maintained.
The employee should not receive any special favors or exemptions from on-the-job rules during treatment.
Managers are given training on how and when to make referrals.

SUPERVISORY TRAINING

For your substance abuse policy and procedures to work, you need to train the supervisors who have daily contact with your employees and are most familiar with their normal behaviors and job performance. The following are topics that should be covered in a supervisory training program.

- The problems that substance abuse causes in general and in the workplace (such as decreased productivity)
- Laws regarding alcohol and drugs
- Types and effects of drugs
- What drug paraphernalia, such as crack pipes, looks like
- Details of the employer's substance abuse policy, procedures, and employee assistance or other program
- Recognition of signs and symptoms of substance abuse (Fig. 6-2) and effects on performance and conduct
- Constructive intervention for an employee with a substance abuse problem
- Implementation of the details and specifics of the employer's substance abuse policy, procedures, and employee assistance or other program
- Problems involved when an employee who has received rehabilitation returns to work

Fig. 6-2 SIGNS AND SYMPTOMS OF SUBSTANCE ABUSE

Physical Appearance

Impaired coordination, unsteady gait, staggering, poor balance
Tremors, shakiness, dizziness, seizures
Impaired muscular control, poor performance of gross or complex motor tasks
Bloodshot eyes, dilated or constricted pupils, watery eyes
Excessive sweating, chills, nausea
Abnormal drowsiness, "nodding off," excessive fatigue, stupor
Blank expression, unresponsiveness
Apparent odor of alcohol on the breath
Inappropriate or bizarre dress, neglect of personal hygiene or appearance

Unusual/Abnormal Behavior

Markedly poor judgment, impulsivity
Carelessness, risk-taking behavior, neglect of safety procedures
Marked irresponsibility, indifference, or rigidity
Marked anxiety, agitation, panic
Mood swings, erratic behavior
Apathy, lethargy, depression, despondency, suicidal thinking
Euphoria, elation, acting "high," excessive talkativeness, overactiveness (restlessness)
Overreactiveness (verbal or physical)—boisterousness, irritability, argumentativeness, quarrelsomeness, belligernace, explosiveness, threats, assaultiveness, combativeness
Slurred speech

Cognitive (Mental) Factors

Inability to concentrate or comprehend, distractibility
Memory deficits, lapses, forgetfulness
Preoccupation, brooding, excessive daydreaming
Confusion, disorientation, incoherence, irrelevancy
Diminished level of consciousness, "out of touch"
Impairment of communication—expressive or receptive
Hallucinations (perceptions that are false/unrealistic)

Source: Cooper, Selden. 1989. The Role of the Line Supervisor or Department Manager in the Employee Assistance Program. Jersey Shore Medical Center. Human Resources Division. Employee Assistance Program. Reprinted with permission.

▪ Confidentiality
▪ Documentation

Certain training methods, such as role-playing, work well in learning how to confront an employee with a substance abuse problem that is impacting job performance. It has been shown that training is more effective when substance abuse professionals, such as law enforcement officials or EAP counselors, take part in the program, and when audiovisuals are used.

EMPLOYEE EDUCATION

Employees need to be educated about the employer's substance abuse policy, procedures, and employee assistance or other program. This is typically done during orientation and, possibly, on a yearly basis for all employees. Employers frequently give employees a policy statement and ask them to sign a form acknowledging that they have each received a copy. Some employers also give employees a general education on drugs that are abused, including the problems they cause.

Attendance Problems

In any given week, one employee out of fifteen is absent from work. The average American employee is absent 7 to 12 times a year, on the average about 9 days. Absenteeism claims 3.2 percent of all scheduled hours. This represents a tremendous cost, not just in wages paid to the absent employees, but in wages for replacement workers as well. Absenteeism also puts an added burden on fellow workers and managers who have to make sure the work gets done. When managers cannot find replacement workers, co-workers are asked to "double up," which they understandably resent. This can lead to job dissatisfaction and poor morale. If the supervisor does manage to find an employee to fill in, it may mean overtime pay and an exhausted, stressed employee.

Hand in hand with concern for absenteeism is a concern for employees' being late to work. When an employee is late for his or her shift, the effects are undoubtedly felt by both co-workers and customers. If problems of absenteeism and lateness get out of hand, the impact on your operation can produce undesirable results.

- Lower quality of customer service
- Low employee morale
- Higher labor costs
- More accidents
- Decreased productivity

You should not accept these problems as facts of life. The situation can be turned around by following the ten commandments of good attendance.

THE TEN COMMANDMENTS OF GOOD ATTENDANCE

1. Keep accurate attendance records.
2. Develop an employee attendance policy and procedure statement that covers *all* employees.
3. Make sure your employees are adequately informed about the attendance policy and the consequences of excessive absenteeism and lateness.
4. Help employees to comply with the attendance policy.
5. Review your employees' attendance records on a regular basis, such as monthly, and provide feedback to employees. Remember, you get what you accept.
6. Reward employees with good attendance records.
7. Promote safety.
8. Be a good role model.
9. Train supervisors to support the program.
10. Make your workplace a great place to work.

Following is a detailed discussion of these steps.

Keeping good attendance records is a prerequisite to tracking your absenteeism and lateness problems. It also helps you to see whether an employee has a pattern of being absent before or after days off or after payday. A pattern of being absent after payday may indicate a substance abuse problem, and you may refer that employee to an employee assistance counselor. Figure 6-3 is a sample attendance record form. The best time to fill in this form is after checking your employees' time cards for payroll purposes.

Good attendance records are critical to defending counseling, warnings, suspensions, and terminations. They are also useful when doing performance appraisals or evaluations.

You need to develop and communicate an employee attendance policy and procedure statement, as seen in Figure 6-4. One major question you

Fig. 6-3 ATTENDANCE RECORD

Name _____

Year _____

	1	2	3	4	5	6	7	8	9	10	11	12	13	14	15	16	17	18	19	20	21	22	23	24	25	26	27	28	29	30	31
JANUARY																															
FEBRUARY																															
MARCH																															
APRIL																															
MAY																															
JUNE																															
JULY																															
AUGUST																															
SEPTEMBER																															
OCTOBER																															
NOVEMBER																															
DECEMBER																															

Reason Code: L—Late to work   V—Vacation   BD—Bonus day   LA—Leave of absense
              S—Called in sick PD—Personal day   F—Funeral day

Fig. 6-4   SAMPLE ATTENDANCE POLICY

ATTENDANCE POLICY

Policy

To meet the needs of our guests as well as fellow employees, regular attendance is a necessity.

Procedure: How to call in late or sick

All employees are expected to contact their immediate supervisors or unit managers 1 hour prior to the scheduled time of reporting if they cannot report to work. All employees are also expected to call in prior to the scheduled time of reporting if they think they will be late to work.

Excessive absenteeism is defined as four or more unscheduled absences from work regardless of reason, including sick time and emergency personal days, in any 3-month period of time.

Excessive lateness is defined as two or more instances of being tardy (more than 10 minutes late) in 1 month.

Disciplinary Action for Excessive Absenteeism and Lateness

A progressive four-step disciplinary process will be followed.

1. Written warning for first offense
2. Second written warning if second offense occurs within 12 months of first written warning
3. Probation period of 90 days if third offense occurs within 12 months of second written warning
4. Termination if an offense occurs during the probation period

If an employee successfully completes the probationary period and another infraction occurs, he or she will be placed back on probation for another 90 days. An employee may be placed on probation only two times during a sliding 24-month period from the date of the first infraction.

---

need to answer before formulating your policy is whether you want to have an excuse-based or no-fault absenteeism policy. In an excuse-based system, there is leniency for absenses with legitimate excuses, such as medical reasons. In a no-fault policy, if employees are absent too many times, they are disciplined regardless of whether or not the absence is legitimately excusable (such as because of illness). This type of program seems to be objective and equitable; it uses progressive discipline and can include some automatic exceptions.

Your attendance policy should

Provide a reasonable definition of excessive absenteeism and lateness

Not be too restrictive in the length of time an employee is given to demonstrate good attendance

Be flexible enough to allow for isolated occurrences

Use progressive discipline

Explain how employees are to contact you when they are going to be late or absent and how much notice you require

Be clear about when you require a doctor's note for an employee to return to work

Be communicated in such a clear manner that the employee is incapable of confusion

New employees should receive a copy of this policy statement upon hire, have it explained, and be asked to sign a copy as documentation for their files.

The purpose of your attendance policy is to *correct*, not to punish, absenteeism and tardiness; therefore, *help employees to comply with the policy.* As with any other policy, employees need to know why good attendance is so important. Tell your employees about the negative effects of excessive absenteeism on their co-workers, overall morale, customers, and profitability.

You can also help employees to comply by addressing absentee issues in a positive way and stressing future improvements rather than past problems. Finally, help employees by offering flexible work schedules, suggestions about available transportation to work, and advice on obtaining child care.

Review your employees' attendance records and give feedback. Employees need to be appropriately disciplined when in violation of policy, as discussed in Chapter 4. When employees exhibit good attendance, they should be rewarded.

There are various ways you can *reward employees for good attendance.* You may use the following or other types of rewards:

Verbal praise
Certificate or plaque (Fig. 6-5)
Time off with pay
Bonus pay
Announcement in newsletter or on bulletin board
Memo or letter (Fig. 6-6)
Article of clothing, perhaps with company logo on it
Cash bonus
Free or reduced-price meal(s)
Free tickets to events
Chances to win a prize
Points toward prizes
A celebration party

Frequent, sincere verbal praise can work wonders in any foodservice operation. Praise can be used to reinforce and shape employees' attitudes toward good attendance. Public praise for accomplishments and contributions is especially powerful. Use these steps to praise your employees' good attendance.

1. Describe the specific action you are praising.
2. Explain the results or effects of the actions.
3. State your appreciation and say thank you.

In addition to praise and recognition, some programs offer a day off with pay for achieving a specified number of weeks or months of perfect attendance. Many employees like this type of program because it offers a tangible, positive incentive not to call in sick. Your employees may also like a program that combines additional time off with a bonus. For instance, you might reward an employee for 1 year of perfect attendance by giving 5 days off and a $200 savings bond.

Employers may also use contests, generally of shorter duration, with prizes to motivate employees toward perfect attendance. To keep employee interest high, the rules and prizes for contests should be changed frequently and designed to suit the employees involved.

Safety hazards in hospitality operations range from knives put into a kitchen sink full of water to hazardous chemicals that housekeepers use to clean hotel rooms. Typical accidents in the hospitality workplace include cuts, falls, burns, and electric shocks. They occur because employees are fooling around, rushing, being careless, working under the influence, not paying attention, or overdoing. Accidents sometimes occur because employees are ignorant or just feel that accidents are inevitable, and so fail to try to prevent them.

Fig. 6-5 GOOD ATTENDANCE CERTIFICATE

Congratulations

Certificate of Good Attendance

This Certificate Is Given to:

_____

on _____

by _____

Fig. 6-6   GOOD ATTENDANCE LETTER

MEMO

TO: Jane Wright, Server
FROM: John Doe, Dining Room Manager
DATE: December 15, 1991
SUBJECT: Good Attendance

I would like to express my appreciation of your good attendance this past quarter. My records indicate that you never called in sick, so you actually had perfect attendance! Congratulations and thank you, on behalf of your co-workers and me. You help make everybody's job a little bit easier every day when you come to work. Keep it up!

All accidents to employees have one thing in common: a person who may incur pain and suffering, financial expenses, and lost work time. Accidents can also lower morale and damage the reputation of the organization. People do cause the majority of accidents, but unsafe working conditions, such as poor lighting, also encourage accidents. Figure 6-7 is an accident prevention guide that can be used to train employees about unsafe practices and can also be posted in work areas as a reminder.

Safety programs are common throughout the hospitality industry and may include some or all of the following components.

- Safety policies and procedures
- Employee training
- Supervision
- Safety Committee
- Inspections for unsafe working conditions and unsafe practices
- Accident reporting and investigation

The more components utilized, the more effective is the safety program.

Safety policies and procedures should be written to cover any situation in which there is potential for an accident. For example, Figure 6-8 shows a procedure for proper lifting. Such policies and procedures form the basis for an employee training program.

Safety training should start at orientation, and all safety information should be put into the employee handbook. The accident rate for employees is higher during the first month of employment than in any subsequent month. Safety training should be repeated once a year for

Fig. 6-7 PREVENTION GUIDE FOR FOODSERVICE SAFETY

PREVENTION GUIDE FOR SAFETY

Preventing Cuts

1. Know how to operate equipment.
2. Pay attention when using sharp equipment. Never touch edge of sharp blades, and wipe away from sharp edges when cleaning.
3. Use guards when provided on equipment.
4. Use tampers to push food into equipment.
5. Turn equipment off before adjusting.
6. Make sure that there are no loose sleeves, ties, or dangling jewelry near equipment.
7. Use knives carefully.
8. Carry dishes and glassware carefully.
9. Sweep up broken glass.
10. Use a special container to dispose of broken glass, dishes, and other sharp objects.
11. Remove nails and staples in shipping cartons and crates, and wear gloves when doing so.
12. Remove can lids entirely from cans and put back into empty cans for disposal.

Preventing Burns

1. Pay attention while working around hot equipment.
2. Use dry pot holders.
3. Keep pot handles turned in from the edge of the range and away from open flames.
4. Avoid overfilling containers with hot foods.
5. Get help for lifting heavy pots of food.
6. Open lids of pots, and doors of steamers, away from you, and do so slowly.
7. Stir foods with long-handled spoons.
8. Warn others of hot surfaces.
9. Let equipment cool before cleaning. Do not use wet rags to clean hot equipment.
10. Do not put icy frozen foods into the fryer. Put foods slowly into the fryer, and stand back.
11. Strike match before turning on gas equipment.
12. Wear closed toe and heel shoes that do not absorb liquids.
13. Wear a cloth apron around hot surfaces; make sure that there are no loose apron strings.

Fig. 6-7 Continued

Preventing Fires

1. Smoke only where allowed.
2. Do not turn your back on hot fat.
3. Keep equipment and hoods free from grease buildup.
4. Do not set the fryer at too high a temperature.
5. Store matches in a covered container away from heat.
6. Keep garbage in covered containers.
7. Store chemicals away from heat.

Preventing Falls

1. Wipe up spills immediately.
2. Use "Wet Floor" signs.
3. Wear shoes with nonskid soles and heels.
4. Keep aisles and stairs clear.
5. Walk, do not run.
6. Follow established traffic patterns.
7. Turn lights on to assure being able to see properly.
8. Do not carry anything that blocks your vision.
9. Keep drawers closed.
10. Use ladders properly. Never stand on a chair, table, or box.
11. Use handrails.
12. Make sure that there are no dangling electric cords.

Preventing Electric Shock

1. Never touch electrical equipment or outlets with wet hands or while standing in water.
2. Unplug equipment before cleaning or disassembling.
3. Do not yank plugs out by their cords.
4. Report damaged and worn plugs and cords to your supervisor.
5. Make sure all electrical equipment is grounded.

Fig. 6-8 PROCEDURE FOR PROPER LIFTING

PROPER LIFTING

1. **Plan it!**

   Do you need help?

   Do you need a cart?

   Where is it going?

2. **Get ready!**

   Squat down with your back straight. Do not bend over from the waist!

   Put one foot alongside the object and one behind it for more stability.

   Grip the object with both hands, one at the bottom corner with palm up, and the other on the opposite top corner.

   Keep arms and elbows close to the body.

   Tuck in your chin.

3. **Lift it!**

   Straighten your knees slowly to stand up, and do not twist your back.

4. **Move it!**

   Keep the object close to you.

   Do not twist your back. If you need to change position, move your feet and entire body.

   Look where you are going.

   Call out "Coming through!" as needed.

5. **Set it down!**

   Do the reverse of Step 3.

   Slide the load into place, watching your fingers and toes.

---

all employees. Topics for safety training can include the causes and prevention of different types of accidents, what to do in case of an emergency, including first aid and the Heimlich maneuver (to stop choking), how to handle hazardous chemicals safely, and how to use and clean equipment properly. Employees also need to know that accidents do not just happen, that they can be prevented. As a part of training, employees need to be evaluated on what they know (see Fig. 6-9) and rewarded or recognized for working safely.

Managers and supervisors can themselves do much to prevent accidents. Besides being responsible for carrying out the various components of the safety program, they can oversee the day-to-day monitoring and enforcement of safety standards, report and correct unsafe conditions, and act as role models. They are vital to creating an environment where safety is practiced and respected.

Safety committees are often formed, which meet periodically to discuss safety matters. The following people may be on a safety committee: managers, supervisors, and employees from various departments, as well as a human resources manager. The safety committee has many functions, such as developing and changing safety policies and procedures, reviewing data on number and types of accidents to date, inspecting the facility, and developing, implementing, and monitoring training.

Inspections of the facility should be made periodically to correct any safety-related problems. In addition to managers and supervisors, employees should take part in the inspection process to encourage them to take a more active role in preventing accidents.

Any accident, no matter how small, should be reported as soon as possible. This is typically accomplished by filling out a standard reporting form (Fig. 6-10). The cause of the accident should be determined in order to take appropriate corrective action. Accident report forms contain much information that can be used in safety training.

Like it or not, you are a *role model* for your employees. If you are late to work frequently and call in sick at least once a month, you should not be surprised if your employees do the same. Employees take their cue from you, the boss. When you are a good role model, you set standards that employees are more apt to adhere to themselves. Figure 6-11 is a checklist of attendance-related behaviors. How do you rate?

Supervisors need to be trained to administer properly this discipline policy, as any other. This topic is discussed in detail in the next chapter.

Many of the tips discussed in the second book in this series, *Retaining Your Foodservice Employees,* can help you *make your workplace a great place to work* for your employees.

Fig. 6-9 EMPLOYEE SAFETY QUIZ

PREVENTING FALLS AND STRAINS QUIZ

Directions: Circle the correct answer.

1. To move two cases of #10 cans from the storeroom to the food preparation area, you should
   a. open the boxes, load your arms with as many cans as possible, and take them to the work area
   b. properly lift and carry one case at a time to the work area
   c. bring a cart with you, and use it
   d. none of the above

2. When lifting a load, you should mainly use your
   a. arm muscles
   b. leg muscles
   c. back muscles

3. You need to lift and move a heavy pot of soup that you are not sure you can handle. You should
   a. flex your muscles and do it yourself
   b. ask for someone to help you lift and move it
   c. split the pot of soup into two pots and then lift and carry each one
   d. any of the above

4. When getting ready to lift a heavy object, you should
   a. lean over from the waist
   b. squat down to the level of the object
   c. squat down as low as you can

5. When getting ready to lift a heavy object, you should
   a. keep your arms, elbows, and the object close to you
   b. keep your arms, elbows, and the object away from your body
   c. do whichever is comfortable

6. When getting ready to lift a heavy object, you should
   a. grab it from the bottom
   b. grab it by the sides
   c. grab it by the bottom corner and the opposite top corner

7. The best material for a shoe's heel and sole so you do not fall on wet floors is
   a. leather
   b. plastic
   c. rubber
   d. none of the above

Fig. 6-9   Continued

8. Describe what to do if a spill occurs.

9. Describe three ways to prevent falls and slips.

10. Show your instructor how to use a stepladder and/or lift properly.

Source: Reprinted from *The Health Care Food Service Training Manual* by K. Drummond with permission of Aspen Publishers, Inc. © 1990.

Tips for Providing a Great Workplace

- Give a friendly greeting to your employees each day and speak with them.
- Actively listen to your employees.
- Give a hand to your employees when appropriate.
- Do not hover over your employees.
- Treat employees fairly and consistently.
- Never discuss an employee's performance with another employee.
- Keep your employees informed.
- Involve your employees.
- When feasible, offer employee counseling and wellness programs.
- Use up-to-date and accurate job descriptions.
- Orient your new employees.
- Train your employees to do their jobs well.
- Coach your employees.
- Formally evaluate employee performance at least once yearly.
- Reward your employees.
- Pay for performance.
- Institute a profit-sharing or other gain-sharing program for employees.
- Help employees see the end result of their work.
- Let your employees make as many of their own decisions as possible.
- Cross-train employees and rotate their positions.
- Give employees special assignments.

Fig. 6-10   SAMPLE ACCIDENT REPORTING FORM

ACCIDENT REPORT FORM

Date of Accident _____   Time of Accident _____
Today's Date   _____

Location of Accident: _____

Description of accident (Include who was involved and what each person
was doing at the time.):

_____

_____

_____

_____

_____

_____

_____

_____

List who was involved in the accident:

Name	Employee or Guest	Describe any injuries and treatment given

List witnesses to the accident:

Name	Employee or Guest	Phone Number

Supervisor's Signature _____   Date _____
General Manager's Signature _____   Date _____

FORWARD ONE COPY TO SAFETY COMMITTEE

Fig. 6-11   SAMPLE FORM FOR RATING ATTENDANCE-RELATED BEHAVIORS

RATE YOUR ATTENDANCE-RELATED BEHAVIORS

Directions: Use the following checklist to help you see whether you are setting a positive example of attendance-related behaviors to your employees.

	Occasionally	Most of the time	Always
1. I am at my desk ready to get to work on time or early.	_____	_____	_____
2. I end my breaks and meal periods on time and get right back to work.	_____	_____	_____
3. I am one of the last people out at the end of my shift.	_____	_____	_____
4. I record my time in and out every day.	_____	_____	_____
5. I park my car where my employees can see it so that they know I am in.	_____	_____	_____
6. When I get to work, I make sure everyone knows I am in.	_____	_____	_____
7. If I am not in my immediate work area, I let someone know.	_____	_____	_____
8. I leave my door open so that everyone knows I am around.	_____	_____	_____
9. I use sick days only when I am really sick.	_____	_____	_____
10. I schedule doctors' appointments on my days off.	_____	_____	_____

- Develop a career ladder and promote from within.
- Offer employees opportunities for personal and professional development.
- Bring in people from the community for tours and cooking classes.
- Be able to perform the jobs you supervise.
- Have competitive and equitable pay rates.
- Offer a competitive benefit package suited to your employees.
- Provide a reasonable work schedule.
- Provide a pleasant, safe, and clean working environment.
- Have fun while you work.

Sexual Harassment

In 1980 Equal Employment Opportunity Commission (EEOC) issued guidelines on sexual harassment, indicating that it is a form of sex discrimination under Title VII of the 1964 Civil Rights Act. The EEOC states that sexual harassment consists of "unwelcome advances, requests for sexual favors, and other verbal or physical conduct of a sexual nature" when compliance with any of these acts is used as a condition of employment. This type of conduct is also considered illegal if it creates an "intimidating, hostile, or offensive working environment." The employer is responsible for preventing the sexual harassment of both female and male employees. Of interest to the foodservice operator is the fact that employers are also guilty if they allow nonemployees, such as guests or individuals making deliveries, to harass employees sexually.

Research shows that perhaps half of all women in the work force experience sexual harassment at some time. In one study of the tourism industry, results showed that sexual harassment is clearly a problem. Of the respondents in this survey, 46 percent reported having been subjected several times to "unwanted teasing, jokes, remarks, or questions of a sexual nature."

If a charge of sexual harassment gets to court, it costs plenty. The employer must pay his or her own legal fees and, in the case of a loss, the victim's legal fees, back pay, lost benefits, interest, and other damages awarded by the court. Other less tangible, but hard-hitting, costs include lowered employee morale, decreased productivity, and possible turnover. If the events gets media coverage, the operation may even lose customers and job applicants.

You, as the employer, are considered guilty of sexual harassment if you knew about or should have known about such misconduct and failed to correct it. If you genuinely did not know that sexual harassment was taking place, liability can be averted if you have an adequate sexual harassment policy and the situation is corrected immediately. If you want to prevent being charged with sexual harassment, it is best to develop and implement a specific sexual harassment policy that includes the following:

An easy-to-understand definition of sexual harassment

Clear-cut disciplinary guidelines for individuals who are guilty of sexual harassment, as well as guidelines for harassers who retaliate against those who turn them in (guidelines should include termination as an option)

A formal complaint procedure for employees to use if they think they have been victims of sexual harassment, with provisions for immediate investigations, prompt disciplinary actions when appropriate, and an alternate path for filing grievances in the event the immediate supervisor may be the harasser

A statement assuring protection for those who make charges and declaring that any retaliatory action against such as employee will not be tolerated

Once a policy is formulated, it needs to be publicized to all concerned. Managers should receive in-depth training on the policy, as well as given information on how to prevent sexual harassment, investigate when charges are made, and follow up with victims after incidents of harassment. Employees also need to be educated about how to recognize sexual harassment and how to confront their harassers. The human resources department is normally involved in this entire process.

7

How to Create a Disciplined
Work Force

Why do employees not do what they are supposed to do? Here are some common reasons.

- *They do not know what to do.* Perhaps employee training was poor or nonexistent or performance standards were not made clear. Before asking an employee to perform a job well and to follow the organization's rules, the manager must communicate all expectations and ascertain that the employee actually does understand them. A well-written job description is a start.
- *They do not know how well they are performing.* Employees need feedback while they are working in order to understand what constitutes appropriate and not so appropriate behavior. A performance management system that has a strong informal review component goes a long way toward making employees aware of their conduct. Positive reinforcement, such as praise, also increases the chances for continued desirable behavior. When managers ignore problem behaviors, they are allowing incompetence, which is then really their fault.
- *They do not know why they are doing a particular task.* If employees understand why a certain task has to be done, or why it should be done a certain way, they are much more likely to do it right.
- *Expectations are unrealistic and unreasonable.* At times, because of job design or lack of supplies or equipment, managers ask employees to do jobs that simply cannot be done. For instance, banquet cooks may be asked to prepare a meal for a certain time that requires more oven space than is available. Subsequently, when there are complaints from a few guests about cold food, the cooking staff is blamed. Expectations may also be unrealistic when an employee is asked to accomplish more than can reasonably be done or to work under poor working conditions.

- *There is a mismatch between the employee and the job.* The employee may be overqualified or underqualified for the job; poor performance can result in either case. Sometimes a foodservice employee who prefers to work alone is hired to work directly with guests. A problem may soon surface and may be blamed on the employee when, in fact, the wrong employee was selected for the position.
- *Finally, employees may not be doing what they are supposed to do because they are not motivated.* The reasons for this can range from laziness or boredom to an inability to see any chance for growth. In some cases, managers can do much to improve an employee's motivational level; in other cases, very little.

In almost all these situations, management can do much to correct the problems.

Eight Ways to Create a Disciplined Work Force

Following are some ways to create a work force of employees who practice self-discipline, rather than employees whom you must discipline on a regular basis.

1. Establish sound selection procedures.
2. Provide a probationary period for all new employees (see Chapter 2).
3. Clearly lay out performance standards and rules of conduct (see Chapter 2).
4. Provide an adequate training program, including employee orientation (see the second book in this series, *Retaining Your Foodservice Employees*).
5. Train supervisors to meet employees' needs and treat employees fairly and consistently.
6. Emphasize mutual respect and communication.
7. Maintain a committed or a positive approach to discipline (see Chapter 1).
8. Ensure due process for employees and just-cause terminations (see Chapters 1 and 5).

In this chapter we will discuss three of these topics: sound selection procedures, training supervisors, and ways to emphasize mutual respect and communication.

Sound Selection Procedures

The first step in evaluating applicants is usually to ask them to fill out an application form. After the initial screening of the application takes place, the applicant should go through further evaluation: interviewing, preemployment testing, and background checks. Keep in mind that no one method used to evaluate or measure applicants does a complete job. Each has its advantages and disadvantages. Useful evaluation methods should be predictive of future job performance, give consistent results, and provide value for time and money spent.

Once an application is completed, it should be screened to determine whether the applicant should go through any further selection procedures. While reviewing applications, ask yourself the following questions, being very careful not to jump to any conclusions, but rather to make notes of questions to ask the applicant to get more information.

Will the writing meet job requirements for legibility, neatness, spelling, and grammar? Did the applicant have someone else fill out the application, and then just sign it? (Check for two styles of handwriting.)

Is there any information that was requested but not provided?

Are there any instructions that were not followed?

How does the applicant's work experience compare with the minimum job requirements? Do previous jobs show preferences for certain types of work?

Do any of the job titles require further explanation?

Does the applicant have a history of changing jobs frequently?

What are the reasons given for changing jobs?

Are there any significant time gaps between jobs?

What is the pattern of the applicant's salary history?

Is there a pattern of increasing job responsibility and pay rates?

How do the applicant's education and training compare with the minimum job requirements?

Preemployment testing may include any of a wide variety of testing devices to help select the best candidate for the job. Performance tests, knowledge tests, psychological tests, and preemployment physical examinations are examples. Tests such as these do not measure the whole person, but rather just one or a few dimensions.

The most common form of background investigation is the reference check, which has several purposes: to make sure the information is not misstated, to provide additional information about the applicant, and to reduce the possibility of being sued for negligent hiring. Most managers prefer checking references by phone because this method yields more useful, candid information and is relatively inexpensive and fast. Be sure to document your phone calls on a reference form that can be used for both verbal and written references (Fig. 7-1). It is best to start your reference check with the human resources or personnel department to verify information such as job titles, dates of employment, and salary history. Always identify yourself and your company and explain that you are doing a reference check.

Next, ask to speak to the applicant's former supervisor. Identify yourself again and tell this person that the information you seek will be held confidential. Start out by confirming objective information such as job titles, attendance record, and so on. Once you feel the former employer will volunteer more information, you can switch from yes-no type questions to those asking for more information. Yet, do not be surprised if this person informs you that he or she will not supply you with any other information than the human resources department has given. Be confident, persistent, and assertive; however, if you get nowhere, this is not unusual.

There are two points to keep in mind when checking references.

- It is more beneficial for the person doing the interview to do the reference checks.
- Always check references of two or more past employers to get a more complete and accurate assessment.

References can also be checked by mail using a form such as Figure 7-2.

Another way to check an employee's background is through the use of public records. Employers can look at criminal records, driving records, workers' compensation records, federal court records, and education records. Information gained from these sources can be used to disqualify an applicant only if the information is job-related and such information is consistently applied in the selection process.

Criminal records are available through either a state central repository or the county. The county tends to be quicker, less costly, and county personnel will often give information on the phone. County information is usually more complete than a state's, but if many counties have to be contacted, it may be easier to contact just the state.

Driving records are available through a state motor vehicle office. Driving records can generally be obtained by mail and are inex-

Fig. 7-1 SAMPLE TELEPHONE REFERENCE CHECK FORM

TELEPHONE REFERENCE CHECK

Applicant Name: _____

Position Applied for: _____

Name of Company, Location, and Phone Number: _____
_____
_____
_____

Name and Title of Person Supplying Reference: _____
_____

1. What are the dates of employment when he or she was employed by you? _____

2. What was his or her title when he or she started working for you, and when he or she left the company? _____
_____

3. What was the starting and ending salary? _____
_____

4. What were his or her primary job duties and responsibilities? _____
_____
_____
_____

5. How much supervision did he or she receive? _____
_____

6. How were his or her attendance and lateness records? _____
_____

7. What was this person's reason for leaving? _____
_____

8. Did he or she do a satisfactory job? _____
_____

9. In what areas were job skills excellent? In what areas were job skills weak? _____
_____

Fig. 7-1 Continued

---

10. Did this individual get along well with others? _____

_____

_____

11. Would you rehire this individual? Why or why not? _____

_____

_____

_____   _____
Date   Name

---

pensive. An employer can use this information to cross-check date of birth, and so forth, for falsification.

Workers' compensation records can reveal whether a candidate has a past history of injuring him- or herself on the job and, if so, whether he or she has been cleared to resume full duties. These records are available through the state.

Unless business necessity can be proved, it is not appropriate to use an applicant's financial status when making an employment decision. There is no evidence that applicants with credit problems will be poor employees or will be more likely to steal. In addition, it is probable that this practice would discriminate against some minority groups.

A final reference source is personal references, if requested on the application. In general, such references offer little productive information, but may have to be contacted if other reference sources do not exist, as in the case of teenagers looking for their first jobs. You may get more insight about an applicant by noting exactly whom he or she listed as personal references.

Following are the primary areas to be discussed during the heart of the interview. They are often discussed in this order, and each area should be completely covered before proceeding.

1. Gather and analyze information about the applicant's knowledge, skills and abilities, work experience, education and training, and personal characteristics.
2. Explain the job fully, including duties, hours of work, overtime

Fig. 7-2   SAMPLE MAIL REFERENCE FORM

MAIL REFERENCE FORM

_____   _____
NAME   SOCIAL SECURITY NUMBER

_____ _____ _____
POSITION   EMPLOYED FROM   TO

    I hereby authorize you to issue any information you may have regarding my services and character and do hereby unconditionally release you from all liability for any damage whatsoever that might result from furnishing this information.

_____ _____
SIGNATURE   DATE

(To be completed by former employer)

    THE ABOVE APPLICANT HAS APPLIED FOR A POSITION. YOUR VERIFICATION OF SERVICE WILL BE APPRECIATED AND KEPT CONFIDENTIAL.

_____ _____ _____
POSITION   EMPLOYED FROM   TO

_____
REASON FOR LEAVING

	YES	NO
Is this individual eligible for rehire?	_____	_____
Did this individual miss more than 5 work days, when they were scheduled to work, in any one of the last 5 years?	_____	_____
During employment with your firm, was this individual ever disciplined or discharged for		
Absenteeism, tardiness, failure to notify your company when absent, or any other attendance-related reasons?	_____	_____
Theft, unauthorized removal of company property, or related offenses?	_____	_____
Fighting, assault, or related offenses?	_____	_____
Being under the influence of alcohol or drugs or for possession, use, or abuse of alcohol or drugs?	_____	_____

Fig. 7-2 Continued

Insubordination?   _____   _____

Violating safety rules?   _____   _____

Unsatisfactory performance?   _____   _____

_____   _____
AUTHORIZED SIGNATURE OF FORMER EMPLOYER   DATE

Source: Jersey Shore Medical Center, Neptune, NJ. Reprinted with permission.

requirements, policies and procedures, wages and benefits, probationary period, performance reviews, training, incentive programs, and growth opportunities. Inform the applicant that he or she will have to provide proof of being able to work in the United States, as well as proof of age if required for the job. Make clear all expectations, including performance standards, if applicable. Give the applicant the job description.
3. Explain the company's goals, history, and structure. Sell the applicant on your company and what it has to offer, being, of course, honest and realistic. Give the applicant any appropriate company information.
4. Ask the applicant whether he or she has anything to add or any questions to ask.

Some interviewers prefer to start the interview by briefly describing the company and/or the job opening. This kind of introduction may help to put the applicant at ease. Others prefer to ask, "Would you tell me what you do (did) in a typical day on the job?" This question allows the applicant to discuss a familiar subject and gives the interviewer a chance to evaluate verbal skills and to get information on which to base further questions.

When reviewing a person's qualifications, be sure to use the questions on the Interviewer's Evaluation Form (Fig. 7-3) as a starting point.

Additional Tips for Interviewing

- Use open-ended, reflective, probing, and situational questions.
- Be nonjudgmental during the entire interview process. Do not jump to conclusions. A poor interviewer reaches a decision in the first 5 minutes.

Fig. 7-3   FORM FOR INTERVIEWER TO EVALUATE APPLICANT

INTERVIEWER'S EVALUATION FORM

Date: _____

Applicant's Name: _____

Position/Department: _____

Job Qualifications	Applicant's Qualifications	Does Not Meet Qualifi-cation	Meets Minimum Qualifi-cation	Exceeds Qualifi-cation
1. Knowledge				
2. Skills and Abilities				
3. Work Experience				
4. Education and Training				

129

Fig. 7-3   Continued

Applicant's Salary Requirements: _____

Can applicant work the schedule or hours required? _____

Level of interest in job: Low   Moderate   High

Overall evaluation: _____ Fails to meet some or all job qualifications

_____ Meets all job qualifications

_____ Exceeds job qualifications

Additional Comments:

_____

_____

_____

_____
Interviewer's Signature

- Recognize your own personal biases and try to not let them influence you. Screen out any ethnocentric thoughts. Be objective. Do not look for clones of yourself. Do not let an applicant's age, sex, attractiveness, or verbal fluency influence your thoughts.
- Spend most of your time listening actively. Allow the candidate to do at least 70 to 80 percent of the talking, and restrict your own talking to 20 to 30 percent at most. Listen to each answer before deciding on the next question. Do not interrupt!
- Make notes openly on the Interviewer's Evaluation Form (Fig. 7-3) so that vital information is not forgotten. Record key points. Explain to the applicant at the beginning of the interview that you will be taking notes to help record information. Most applicants will not mind this, as they want you to remember as much about them as possible.
- Repeat or paraphrase the applicant's statements to ascertain better understanding and get more information. You might say something such as, "So you were responsible for the dining room staff in that job . . ." or repeat, with a questioning inflection, the applicant's last few words. Periodically summarize the applicant's statements to clarify points and bring information together. A

summary statement may begin with, "Let's state the major points up to now," thus allowing the applicant to confirm or clarify what has been discussed. Paraphrasing and summarizing are also good techniques to get an applicant talking and show interest.

- Another technique used to get a quiet applicant talking and show interest is to provide pauses to allow the applicant to sense that more information is desired and possibly feel more compelled to talk. During this time you can observe the applicant's poise. Using certain phrases such as "I see," "How interesting," and "I didn't know that" also encourages talking. Any phrases used should indicate interest, not agreement or disagreement. Avoid agreeing or disagreeing.
- Use body language to show interest and elicit information. Use direct eye contact, nod, smile, and lean slightly forward.
- Do not be hesitant to probe for more information when it is called for, such as when an applicant talks very briefly or vaguely about an important topic. Most applicants do not want to discuss a bad experience they have had. If unfavorable information is revealed, make a comment such as "That happens to all of us at one time or another" to defuse the situation. You should wait until the latter part of the interview to discuss any concerns you may have about the applicant.
- Paint a realistic picture of the job. Be honest. Make no promises you cannot keep, and provide information freely. Young people looking for their first job often have unrealistic expectations and need to know about a job's drawbacks, such as night and weekend hours. Painting a realistic job picture reduces employee dissatisfaction and turnover.
- Speak in language that the applicant will understand.
- Always be sincere, respectful, courteous, and friendly. Treat all applicants the same.

After using these techniques to evaluate applicants, it is time to make the selection. The goal, when making the selection, is to pick the best person for the job. This is not usually a simple task. The selection of an applicant must be based on the person's knowledge, skills and abilities, work experience, education and training, and personal characteristics as they relate to the job qualifications. Any criteria used in the selection process must be consistently and directly related to job performance.

Using the Comparison of Applicants for Selection form (Fig. 7-4), you can compare the various applicants. Selection can be complicated because the best candidate, as identified by one method, such as

Fig. 7-4 FORM TO COMPARE APPLICANTS FOR SELECTION

COMPARISON OF APPLICANTS FOR SELECTION

Date: _____

Position/Department to be filled: _____

First, fill in the job qualifications for this position. Next, rate each applicant using this scale:

1   Does not meet qualification
2   Meets minimum qualification
3   Exceeds qualification

	Applicant	Applicant	Applicant	Applicant
Job Qualifications				
1. Knowledge				
2. Skills and Abilities				
3. Work Experience				
4. Education and Training				

Fig. 7-4 Continued

Rate each applicant using this scale.

    1   Unsatisfactory results

    2   Satisfactory results

    3   Above average results

	Applicant	Applicant	Applicant	Applicant
Preemployment Testing				
Test 1				
Test 2				
Test 3				
Test 4				
Background Checks				
Reference 1				
Reference 2				
Reference 3				
Reference 4				
Reference 5				
Totals				

Final Selection: _____

Name of Person(s) Making Selection: _____

_____

preemployment testing, may not be the best candidate as indicated by another method, such as interviewing. This form helps to give you the total picture.

Tips for Making a Selection

- Every job requires a worker to function in some degree in relation to people, data, and things. For jobs that require direct customer contact, be sure to select applicants who enjoy being with people. Applicants who prefer to work with numbers may prefer purchasing or accounting work. Applicants who like to work with food or other supplies may be best for taking care of storage areas or cooking.
- When the best candidate for a job is overqualified, there is often concern that this individual will be bored or unproductive and will leave the job when a better opportunity comes up. This is not always the case; it depends on the candidate's motivation to take the job and whether he or she may be moved into a higher position fairly quickly. Each situation should be looked at individually.

Trained Supervisors

Discipline is not a science with clear-cut rules that are easily applied. It is a management skill that can be learned with sufficient training and experience. Supervisors need to be trained on the following discipline-related topics.

- The meaning, purpose, and process of discipline
- How to be fair and consistent
- How to develop performance standards and expectations
- How to coach employees
- How to prepare performance appraisals and conduct performance appraisal interviews
- How to handle incidents of misconduct
- How to identify employees in need of an employee assistance program
- When termination is appropriate and how to conduct a termination interview
- How to document
- How to reduce employee defensiveness
- How to communicate
- Motivation

Supervisors should be trained preferably through teaching methods such as role-playing (for instance, role-playing a performance appraisal interview) and written exercises (filling out disciplinary action forms). These methods help them to practice new behaviors. The Appendix to this book contains a sample outline for a supervisory training class.

One method that helps train supervisors to both reinforce positive behaviors as well as confront inappropriate behaviors involves a regular supervisory problem-solving session. During this session each supervisor is asked to present one employee issue for group discussion. The issue may concern an employee who is having a problem with adhering to the operation's code of conduct or one who is doing a good job and needs reinforcement. This type of meeting reduces supervisory tension in regard to discipline, increases the chance of supervisors dealing with poor performance or misconduct issues instead of sweeping them under the rug, and increases the frequency of recognizing and praising employees.

In addition to training, supervisors need to be involved in creating or revising the discipline system. All too often supervisors are forced to follow discipline or corrective action policy and procedures that they did not create or influence. Whether they like it or not, they must use this policy to guide their actions. Many in this situation make it obvious to the employees they discipline that "they made me do it." This attitude undermines the discipline system as well as the employee's respect for the supervisor and the system. Your supervisors need to have a say in your discipline or corrective action policy and procedures, perhaps during a periodic policy review and revision, in order for them to believe in and implement policy and procedures appropriately.

Emphasis on Mutual Respect and Communication

To create an environment in which employees take responsibility for their own actions, you need to emphasize mutual respect and good communication.

Strategies for Increasing Mutual Respect and Caring

- Catch people doing things right.
- Treat your employees the way you would want to be treated.
- Offer positive reinforcements. Treat your employees as the stars they are.

- Provide opportunities for socializing, such as trips and company teams.
- Manage performance properly.
- Make sure job pressures are reasonable.
- Set a good example: be honest, trusting, sincere, caring, fair, consistent, and decisive.
- Post position openings and promote as much as possible from within.
- Set in place a career ladder.
- Provide immediate and relevant feedback.
- Allow your employees to be involved in relevant decision making.
- Actively solicit constructive suggestions.
- Involve employees through such means as consultive management, work committees or quality circles, suggestion programs, team building, or employee ownership/profit-sharing plans.
- Maintain a safe and pleasant physical work environment.
- Do not cause excessive fatigue, boredom, stress, and/or frustration.

Guidelines for Good Communication

- Maintain close communication between management and employees, both upward and downward.
- Communicate all expectations, including those concerning performance, discipline, evaluation, rewards, and organizational goals, policies, and procedures.
- Communicate to each employee how his or her job and tasks fit into the organization.
- Communicate the importance of quality and service to guests.
- Inform employees in advance of changes and explain why change is necessary.
- Provide means for employees to express their opinions, to complain, and to get a response.
- Actively listen to your employees.

Appendix

Communicating Effectively

LEARNING OBJECTIVES

Upon completing this training session, the employee will be able to

1. explain the process and purpose of communication
2. discuss an advantage and a disadvantage of different communication mediums
3. describe the nature of formal and informal communication
4. apply the guidelines for effective communication

HANDOUTS

1. Class Outline
2. Quiz

TIME REQUIRED 45–75 minutes

EVALUATION

1. Written Quiz
2. Coaching

Key Concepts	Trainer's Directions

WARMUP AND INTRODUCTION

Introduction	Introduction Exercise
Warm-up Questions 1. What percentage of your time is spent communicating both verbally and in writing?	• Pass out Handout #1, "Class Outline." Ask managers to answer the Warm-up Questions. (There are no right or wrong an-

---

*Reprinted from The Health Care Food Service Training Manual by K. Drummond with permission of Aspen Publishers, Inc., © 1990.

Key Concepts	Trainer's Directions
2. What communication methods or mediums, such as meetings, do you use to communicate to those people who are above you and below you? What types of information must you communicate? 3. How important is listening in the communication process? 4. Describe an on-the-job situation in which you thought you communicated well, and the results of that communication. 5. Describe two positive aspects of your communication skills, and two areas you would like to work on.	swers.) Then ask managers to discuss their responses briefly. Explain that today the class will help everyone to communicate better, both within and outside the department.
	• Explain learning objectives.

LEARNING OBJECTIVES

Learning Objective 1

The employee will be able to explain the process and purpose of communication.

Communication is the process of passing along information and understanding from one individual or group to another. In managing, probably more than 50 percent of your time is spent in communicating. Not only is *what* you communicate important, but *how* it is communicated is also crucial.

Lecture/Guided Discussion
• Define *communication*.

Key Concepts	Trainer's Directions

The communication process is a series of steps involving a sender, a message, and a receiver.

- *The sender* puts an idea into words and transmits it to the receiver, who perceives and evaluates the message, and responds.
- *The receiver* has a perceptual filter through which messages are interpreted, and possibly misinterpreted. How the message gets across also depends on the sender's attitude, perceptions, goals, communication skills, and methods used.
- *Messages* are conveyed by using words, either written or spoken, or are conveyed without words, in the case of nonverbal communication. Nonverbal communication includes thoughts and ideas communicated through the use of the voice, body, physical distance, or dress.

- Ask managers for the three components (sender, message, receiver) of the communication process. Write them on a board or easel pad. Describe the process.

Foodservice Managers Communicate
- Praise
- Evaluation of performance
- Policies and procedures
- Goals and objectives
- Any operational changes

- Ask managers for examples of what they communicate during a typical workday.

Possible Effects of Poor Communication
- Poor morale
- Frustration

- Ask managers to describe briefly what happens when there is poor communication in your department. List the ef-

Key Concepts	Trainer's Directions
• Poor service • High turnover of employees • Low productivity • Increased number of accidents • Increased costs The *purpose* of communication is to provide both the knowledge and understanding for effort, and the attitudes needed for employee motivation and cooperation. In short, communication provides your employees with the will to work.	fects on a board or easel pad. Be sure to cover all Key Concepts. • Finally, explain the purpose of communication and emphasize how good communication can reverse the effects of poor communication just discussed.

Learning Objective 2

The employee will be able to discuss an advantage and a disadvantage of different communication mediums.

Lecture/Guided Discussion
- Ask managers to give you examples of different communication mediums. Write on a board or easel pad.
- Next, ask for specific advantages and disadvantages of each one and write down.
- Be sure to cover all Key Concepts.

Advantages and Disadvantages of Different Communication Mediums (see below)

Medium	Advantages	Disadvantages
One-on-one Discussion	• Provides immediate feedback • Can be informal • Focuses message • Includes nonverbal messages	• Not always possible or practical • Can be time-consuming as the result of small talk or having to gather employees together

Key Concepts		Trainer's Directions
Telephone call	• Readily available • Offers verbal contact with people at a distance • Can be quick	• Fewer nonverbal cues than in-person discussion • Can be time-consuming as a result of difficulty in getting person on the phone and possibility of small talk
Meeting	• Gets message to many people at one time • Can provide good feedback • Can involve participants • Gives feeling of belonging • Saves time	• If poorly handled, can be a waste of time • May be impersonal
Memo or letter	• Can be well thought out and organized • Provides documentation	• No immediate feedback • Time-consuming • Greater possibility for misunderstanding than verbal communication
Posted notice	• Quick • Designed to reach many people	• May not be read • No immediate feedback

Learning Objective 3

The employee will be able to describe the nature of formal and informal communication.

Formal communication occurs along the lines of authority found in the department's organizational chart. It can occur in three different directions: upward, downward, or laterally.

Lecture/Guided Discussion

• Ask managers to explain the difference between formal and informal communication. Explain the nature of formal communication and its three aspects, and ask for examples of

Key Concepts	Trainer's Directions
1. *Upward communication* is communication between an employee and his or her boss. Examples: suggestion box, grievances, employee morale or satisfaction survey, management-employee meetings, exit interviews.	upward and downward communication. Write on a board or easel pad. Explain informal communication.
2. *Downward communication* is communication between any superior and subordinate. Examples: policies and procedures, employee handbook, bulletin boards, job descriptions, newsletters, employee meetings.	
3. *Lateral communication* is communication between people at the same level within an organization.	

Informal communication occurs without regard to an individual's place in the organization, authority, or job; often called "the grapevine"; it is important for managers to listen to the grapevine, but to recognize also that it sometimes spreads false rumors.

Learning Objective 4

The employee will be able to apply the guidelines for effective communication.

	Buzz Groups/Lecture/Role Play
Barriers to Communication	• Ask managers to break into groups of two or three and write down what they consider to be barriers to communication.
• Differences between individuals	
• Poor choice of words	

Key Concepts	Trainer's Directions
• Poor choice of communication medium • Poor listening skills • Lack of honesty • Lack of trust • Lack of concern and sincerity • Defensive or hostile attitude • Lack of feedback • Bad timing • Inability to find the time • Disorganization • Noise or other distractions	Give them 5 minutes to complete the exercise. Ask one person from each group to report back the group's answers. Write them on a board or easel pad. Be sure to cover all Key Concepts.

Guidelines for
Effective Communication

1. Be honest, sincere, trusting, open-minded, empathetic, tactful, responsive, and knowledgeable when communicating. Have a sense of humor and keep your emotions in line.
2. Communicate what others need to know, and do it on a timely basis, using appropriate communication channels and mediums.
3. State the message specifically and directly.
4. Show consideration and respect for the person with whom you are communicating. Explain "why" when appropriate.
5. Give and ask for feedback in order to increase understanding.
6. Think, plan, and organize what you want to communicate.

• Review the Guidelines for Effective Communication.

Key Concepts	Trainer's Directions
7. Concentrate on the issues being communicated, not the personalities. 8. Use active listening by • Concentrating on what the speaker is saying • Looking at the speaker • Listening for major points • Reacting to ideas, not to persons • Not jumping to conclusions • Asking questions at appropriate times • Restating major points to confirm understanding 9. When speaking, be aware of your nonverbal communication and make sure your tone of voice, body language, etc., work with, not against, your message. 10. When writing • Be concise and clear • Identify the purpose of the communication at its beginning • Organize the contents well • Be neat	
Role Plays 1. An employee has asked you, the supervisor, for next Friday off, using the proper procedure. You cannot give him or her the day off because you have already given the day off to another person and to do so would result in short staffing.	• Ask the group to break into smaller groups of three and to select one of the role-play situations. Two of the three people will each act out a role while the third person observes. After the role play is completed, have the group evaluate the effectiveness of the communication. This pro-

Key Concepts	Trainer's Directions
You need to give an answer to the employee, who you know will be upset.	cess can be repeated to allow observers to take roles.

2. The lunch meal is just ending in the cafeteria, and you notice that a server is serving huge portions of the entrée. You need to correct this situation for the second time in a week.
3. As a production manager, you need to communicate to your head cook that you want the cooks to cook two menu items (macaroni and cheese, beef stew) from scratch. Both dishes had previously been purchased ready prepared. The head cook will need to be persuaded.

SUMMARY

Summary Exercise
- Ask managers to complete the "Personal Communication Goals" section of their Class Outline (Handout #1).
- Pass out Handout #2, the Quiz, and ask managers to complete and hand it in.

Communicating Effectively
Handout #1

Class Outline

I. Learning Objectives
1. Explain the process and purpose of communication.
2. Discuss an advantage and a disadvantage of different communication mediums.
3. Describe the nature of formal and informal communication.
4. Apply the guidelines for effective communication.

II. Warm-up Questions
1. What percentage of your time is spent communicating both verbally and in writing?
2. What communication methods or mediums, such as meetings, do you use to communicate to those people who are above you and below you? What types of information must you communicate?
3. How important is listening in the communication process?
4. Describe an on-the-job situation in which you thought you communicated well, and results of that communication.
5. Describe two positive aspects of your communication skills, and two areas you would like to work on.

III. Process and Purpose of Communication
1. Communication is the process of passing along information and understanding from one individual or group to another.
2. Communication involves a sender, a message, and a receiver.
3. Both the sender and the receiver have perceptual filters through which messages are interpreted or misinterpreted.
4. Possible effects of poor communication include (fill in response).
5. The purpose of communication is to provide both the knowledge and understanding for effort, and the attitudes needed for employee motivation and cooperation.

146

IV. Advantages and Disadvantages of Different Communication Mediums
   1. One-on-one
   2. Discussion
   3. Telephone call
   4. Meeting
   5. Memo or letter
   6. Posted notice

V. Formal and Informal Communication
   1. Formal communication occurs along the lines of authority found in the department's organizational chart. It can occur upward, downward, or laterally.
      • Upward communication

      • Downward communication

      • Lateral communication

   2. Informal communication occurs without regard to an individual's place in the organization, authority, or job. It is often called "the grapevine."

VI. Barriers to Communication

VII. Guidelines for Effective Communication
   1. Be honest, sincere, trusting, open-minded, empathetic, tactful, responsive, and knowledgeable when communicating. Have a sense of humor and keep your emotions in line.

2. Communicate what others need to know, and do it on a timely basis, using appropriate communication channels and mediums.
3. State the message specifically and directly.
4. Show consideration and respect for the person with whom you are communicating. Explain "why" when appropriate.
5. Give and ask for feedback in order to increase understanding.
6. Think, plan, and organize what you want to communicate.
7. Concentrate on the issues being communicated, not the personalities.
8. Use active listening by concentrating on what the speaker is saying, looking at the speaker, listening for major points, reacting to ideas and not to persons, not jumping to conclusions, asking questions at appropriate times, and restating major points to confirm understanding.
9. When speaking, be aware of your nonverbal communication and make sure your tone of voice, body language, etc., work with, not against, your message.
10. When writing, be concise and clear, identify the purpose of the communication at its beginning, organize the contents well, and be neat.

VIII. Role Plays
1. An employee has asked you, the supervisor, for next Friday off, using the proper procedure. You cannot give him or her the day off because you have already given the day off to another person and to do so would result in short staffing. You need to give an answer to the employee, who you know will be upset.
2. The lunch meal is just ending in the cafeteria, and you notice that a server is serving huge portions of the entrée. You need to correct this situation for the second time in a week.
3. As a production manager, you need to communicate to your head cook that you want the cooks to cook two menu items (macaroni and cheese, beef stew) from scratch. Both dishes had previously been purchased ready prepared. The head cook will need to be persuaded.

IX. Personal Communication Goals

Directions: Write below one or two personal communication skills that you would like to improve. Next, write down a goal you will use as a guide to improve each skill.

   Sign your name below, signifying that you are going to work toward these goals.

1. Personal Communication Skill to Improve:

   Goal:

2. Personal Communication Skill to Improve:

   Goal:

_____   _____

EMPLOYEE SIGNATURE   DATE

Communicating Effectively
Handout #2

Quiz

1. Explain briefly the process and purpose of communication.

2. List four different communication mediums and give an advantage and a disadvantage for each one.

3. What is the difference between formal and informal communication?

4. Given the following situation, discuss how you would apply the four guidelines for effective communication.

   You are in charge of the dining room. After much thought and input from your employees, you have decided that you need to change their schedules to have them come in 30 minutes later and leave 30 minutes later as well. You feel strongly that this will improve productivity and provide better service for the guests, but you know the employees will resist this change.

Bibliography

Asherman, Ira G., and Sandra Lee Vance. 1981. Documentation: A tool for effective management. *Personnel Journal* 60(8):641–43.

Balfour, Alan. 1984. Five types of non-union grievance systems. *Personnel* 61(2):67–76.

Bockanic, William N., and J. Benjamin Forbes. 1986. The erosion of employment-at-will: Managerial implications. *SAM Advanced Management Journal* 51(3):16–21.

Boyle, Kathy. 1987. Effective employee discipline requires keeping in close touch. *Restaurants USA* 7(10):26–28.

Brown, Maurice. 1986. Counseling skills. *SAM Advanced Management Journal* 51(1):32–35.

Bryant, Alan W. 1984. Replacing punitive discipline with a positive approach. *Personnel Administrator* 29(2):79–87.

Buckman, Steve. 1986. To fire or not to fire? *Supervisory Management* 31(2):30–33.

Cameron, Dan. 1984. The when, why and how of discipline. *Personnel Journal* 63(7):37–39.

Campbell, David N., R. L. Fleming, and Richard C. Grote. 1985. *Harvard Business Review* 63(4):162–76.

Condon, Thomas J. 1985. Use union methods in handling grievances. *Personnel Journal* 64(1):72–75.

Connolly, Paul M. 1986. Clearing the deadwood. *Training and Development Journal* 40(1):58–60.

Corbett, Laurence P. 1986. Avoiding wrongful discharge suits. *Management Solutions* 31(6):19–23.

Filipowski, Diane. 1991. Perspectives: Is pay linked to performance? *Personnel Journal* 70(5):39.

Flynn, Kelly. 1991. Preventive Medicine for sexual harassment. *Personnel* 68(3):17.

Foxman, Loretta D., and Walter L. Polsky. 1991. HR skills help managers turn around poor performers. *Personnel Journal* 70(5):28–31.

Geber, Beverly. 1988. The hidden agenda of performance appraisals. *Training* 26(6):42–44, 46–47.

Granholm, Axel R. 1991. *Handbook of Employee Termination.* New York: John Wiley & Sons, Inc.

Griffith, T. J. 1987. Want job improvement? Try counseling. *Management Solutions* 32(9):13–19.

Guinn, Kathleen A., and Roberta J. Corona. 1991. *Personnel Journal* 70(5): 72–79.

Harvey, Eric L. 1987. Discipline vs. punishment. *Management Review* 76(3):25–29.

Hilgert, Raymond L. 1988. How at-will statements hurt employers. *Personnel Journal* 67(2):75–76.

Humphreys, L. Wade, and Neil J. Humphreys. 1988. The proper use of discipline. *Management Solutions* 33(5):5–10.

Lo Bosco, Maryellen. 1985. Nonunion grievance procedures. *Personnel* 62(1):61–64.

Long, Johnny, and Joseph G. Ormsby. 1987. Stamp out absenteeism. *Personnel Journal* 66(11):94–96.

Lowe, Terry R. 1986. Eight ways to ruin a performance review. *Personnel Journal* 65(1):60–62.

Madsen, Roger B., and Barbara Knudson-Fields. 1987. Productive progressive discipline procedures. *Management Solutions* 32(5):17–24.

Matejka, J. Kenneth, D. Neil Ashworth, and Diane Dodd-McCue. 1986. Discipline without guilt. *Supervisory Management* 31(5):34–36.

McCarthy, Joseph P. 1991. A new focus on achievement. *Personnel Journal* 70(2):74–76.

McConnell, Patrick L. 1986. Is your discipline process the victim of RED tape? *Personnel Journal* 65(3):64–71.

Milbourn, Gene. 1986. The case against employee punishment. *Management Solutions* 30(11):40–43.

National Restaurant Association. 1987. *Substance Abuse and Employee Assistance Programs*. Washington D.C.: National Restaurant Association.

Nobile, Robert J. 1991. The law of performance appraisals. *Personnel* 68(1):7.

Plachy, Roger J. 1988. *Performance Management*. New York: AMACOM.

Pulich, Marcia Ann. 1986. What to do with incompetent employees. *Supervisory Management* 31(3):10–16.

Recker, W. A. 1987. The ten commandments of firing. *Management Solutions* 32(5):42–43.

Redeker, James R. 1989. *Employee Discipline: Policies and Practices*. Washington D.C.: BNA Books.

Sandwich, Paul. 1987. Absenteeism: You get what you accept. *Personnel Journal* 66(11):88–93.

Schaffer, Robert H. 1991. Demand better results—and get them. *Harvard Business Review* 69(2):142–49.

Schuster, Karolyn. 1988. Wyse's company manners, the touch management jobs: How to criticize and fire with style. *Food Management* 23(6):210.

Seltzer, Joseph. 1987. Discipline with a clear sense of purpose. *Management Solutions* 32(2):32–37.

Sherman, Clayton. 1987. Eight steps to preventing problem employees. *Personnel* 64(6):38–48.

Steiner, Julius. 1988. Good supervision: The best defense against wrongful discharge claims. *Management Solutions* 33(7):28–31.

Stone, Florence M. (ed.). 1989. *The AMA Handbook of Supervisory Management.* New York: AMACOM.

Straub, Joseph T. 1991. Disciplinary interviews: The buck stops with you. *Supervisory Management* 36(4):1–2.

Thompson, Robert, Jr. 1990. *Substance Abuse and Employee Rehabilitation.* Washington D.C.: BNA Books, 4–7, 67–70.

Tylczak, Lynn. 1990. *Attacking absenteeism.* Los Altos: Crisp Publications, Inc.

Veglahn, Peter A. 1987. The five steps in practicing effective discipline. *Management Solutions* 32(11):24–35.

Zemke, Ron. 1985. Is performance appraisal a paper tiger? *Training* 22(12):24.

INDEX

Accident reports, 114
  sample form, 117
Accuracy in warnings to
    employees, 68
Addiction versus abuse, 92
Age Discrimination in Employment
    Act of 1967, and discharge
    decisions, 82
Alcohol abuse, and performance of
    employees, 91–92
Alternatives to dismissal, 78, 81
Americans with Disabilities Act of
    1990, and discharge
    decisions, 82
Anger, and deferred action, 42, 70
Appeal of disciplinary decisions, 12
  See also Grievance procedure
Application form, 123
Arbitration of grievances, 30
Arrests/convictions, off-duty, 96–97
Association of Labor-Management
    Administrators and
    Consultants, 99
Attendance
  policy for, example, 106
  problems with, 103–108
  record of, 104
    example, 105

self-evaluation form for
    managers, 118

Back pay, awards in wrongful
    discharge judgments, 71
Behavior, focus on, 38
  in warnings to employees, 68
Benefits
  of suitable discipline, 1–2
  terminated employees', 76, 78
Body language
  in active listening, 36
  in an interview, 131
Buzz groups for supervisors'
    training, 142

Central tendency, error of, 52
Checklist
  for performance improvement, 59
  for signs of substance abuse, 102
  for solutions to problem
      behavior, 64
  for a termination interview,
      86–87
Civil Rights Act of 1964
  and discharge decisions, 81
  and employment-at-will, 72

(*continued*)
  sex discrimination as defined in,
    119
Clearance procedures for
    terminated employees, 78
Coaching, 2, 13, 38–43
  formal, 40–43
  informal, 40
  listening skills for, 35–37
  by a supervisor, 6
COBRA. *See* Consolidated Omnibus
    Budget Reconciliation Act
Code of conduct, 2
  development of, 13, 14, 19
  in an employee handbook, 33
  example, 20
Commitment of employees, and
    positive discipline, 6
Communicating effectively,
    supervisors' training in
  handouts for, 146–149
  outline of, 137–145
Communication
  of a drug policy, 92
  education about the employer's
    substance abuse policy, 103
  of an employee attendance policy,
    104, 106–107
  of expectations, 13–33
  guidelines for, 136
  improving with performance
    appraisals, 46
  of performance standards, 2
  of a sexual harassment policy,
    120
  of a substance abuse policy, 98
Comparison of Applicants for
    Selection form, 131–133
Complaint procedure for sexual
    harassment, 120
Concerns procedure. *See* Grievance
    procedure
Conduct rules, clear identification
    of, 11
Conduct rule violations, 61–70
  resolving with progressive
    discipline, 9

Confidentiality of employee
    assistance programs, 100
Confrontation of poor performance,
    41–42
Consent form for drug testing, 98
Consistency, guidelines for
    maintaining, 26
Consolidated Omnibus Budget
    Reconciliation Act (COBRA)
    of 19, 76, 78
  letter covering obligations under,
    example, 79
Contracts, implied legally
    enforceable, 72–73
Cookbook approach, specified
    penalty for every
    infraction, 19
Corrective actions, 135
  development of a policy for,
    19–32
  documentation in code of conduct
    infractions, 68
  guidelines for, 37
  timeliness and effectiveness of, 70
Cost, financial, of substance
    abuse, 92
Counseling
  to discuss conduct rule
    violations, 9
  documentation in a supervisor's
    log, 66
  See also Coaching
County court records, and reference
    checks, 124
Credit references, appropriate use
    of, 126
Criminal records, reference checks
    of, 124

Decision by the employee to engage
    in misconduct, 13
Decision day
  defined, 6
  for reviewing resolutions of rule
    violations, 9–10
Defamation of character, and
    written references, 78

Defensiveness, reducing
employee's, 38
Dehiring, 78, 81
Demotion, 78, 81
Discharges, rules covering, 75–76
Disciplinary actions
example of explicit, 17–19
for sexual harassment, 120
Disciplinary interview, 62–64
Discipline, 1–12
approaches to, 4–6
defined, 1
flow chart, 25
selecting a process for, 21
Disciplined work force, 121–136
Documentation
of accident reports, 114
during applicant screening, 123
of attendance records, 104
of coaching, 43
of a disciplinary interview, 64
in the discipline process, 11
of failure to meet performance
standards, 57
of a first counseling session for
conduct rule violations, 9
mail reference form, 127–128
of meetings with employees, 65–68
of phone calls for reference
checking, 124
policy for removing from files,
27–28
of solutions, conduct rule
violations, 9
example, 10
telephone reference check form,
125–126
of a termination interview, 89
See also Forms; Logbooks
Driving records as reference checks,
124
Drug abuse and performance of
employees, 92. *See also*
Alcohol abuse; Substance
abuse
Drug Free Workplace Act of
1988, 92

Drug testing, 98
Due process, 11–12
assuring on termination, 83–84
to avoid litigation and
unionization, 75
and confrontation with a
problem, 62–63
and employee satisfaction, 73, 75
Duties and responsibilities, spelling
out in performance
standards, 15–16

EAP. *See* Employee assistance
program
EEOC. *See* Equal Employment
Opportunity Commission
Effective communication
guidelines for, 143–144
personal goals for, self-evaluation,
149
Emotional distress damages,
awards in wrongful discharge
judgments, 71
Emotional responses, reacting to
during a termination
interview, 88
Empathy, 38
Employee assistance program
(EAP), 93, 99–101
description in a substance abuse
policy statement, 94–95
voluntary referral to, 98
Employee communication
procedure. *See* Grievance
procedure
Employee expectations, 11–12
Employee handbook, 33
statements on job security in, 73
Employee incident record, verbal
warning documentation,
example, 67
Employee Retirement Income
Security Act (ERISA) of
1974, 78
and discharge decisions, 82
Employees, improvement
documentation, 65

Employee training, and employee
failure to perform to
expectations, 121
Employer responsibility for failures
beyond an employee's
control, 13
Employment-at-will
doctrine of, 72–75
statements intended to
safeguard, 74
Equal Employment Opportunity
Commission (EEOC),
guidelines for sexual
harassment prevention, 119
ERISA. *See* Employee Retirement
Income Security Act
Evaluation
criteria listed in performance
standards, 15–16
interviewer's form for, 129–130
rating categories, 47–52
Evidence of conduct rule violations,
61–62
Excuse-based attendance policy,
107
Exempt employees, 19
Exercising a legal right, exception
to employment-at-will, 72
Expectations
communication of, 33
establishment of, 13–33
Extenuating circumstances in
conduct rule violations,
61–62

Fact-finding, 70
before corrective action, 61
and a decision about disciplinary
actions, 65
in the discipline process, 11
reviewing in a disciplinary
interview, 63
in suspension and possible
discharge, 76
Federal court records for reference
checks, 124

Feedback
in assessing attendance problems,
107
to assure employee compliance,
121
from employees during appraisal
review, 55, 56
during performance appraisals,
46
on performance through
coaching, 39–40
in the traditional approach to
discipline, 4–5
Filing for workers' compensation,
and discharge decisions, 82
First-aid training, 114
First impression error, 53–54
Fixed impression error, 53–54
Flexibility
in attendance policies, 107
in evaluating conduct rule
violations, 61–62
and fairness, 26
Follow-up
of counseling, 9
of a disciplinary interview, 64
Forms
for accident reports, 117
for attendance self-evaluation,
118
for comparison of applicants for
selection, 132–133
graphic rating scale, 52
for grievances, 31–32
for an incident record, 45
for an interviewer's evaluation,
129–130
for notice to a marginal
employee, 58
for performance appraisal, 48–51
for separation, 80
for reference checks, 125, 127
for a warning notice, 69
See also Logbook; Checklist
Front pay, awards in wrongful
discharge judgments, 71

Generalization of standards, statement in policy, 27
Goals, comparison of traditional and positive disciplinary approach, 7
Good attendance recognition certificate, 109
letter, 110
Graphic rating scale, example, 52
Grievance procedure, 28–32
considerations in selecting, 21
form, example, 31–32
informing an employee about, 64
for sexual harassment by a supervisor, 120
Guidelines
for active listening, 36, 38
for assuring good attendance, 104
for a better workplace, 116
for coaching, 42–43
for conducting a disciplinary interview, 63–64
for conducting a termination interview, 89
for creating a disciplined work force, 122
for developing a discipline policy, 21
for disciplinary or corrective action, 26–28
for discipline for sexual harassment, 120
for documenting disciplinary action, 66–68
for effective communication, 143–144, 147–148
for fact-finding, 61
for food service safety, 111–113
for interviewing, 128, 130–131
for performance appraisal, 47, 55–56
for preparing for a performance appraisal, 55
for reviewing termination for just cause, 83–84

for a step grievance procedure, 29–32
for successful employee assistance programs, 101

Halo effect, 52
Hazardous chemicals, training in handling, 114
Head cook, performance standards, 15–19
Health insurance of terminated employees, 76, 78
Heimlich maneuver, 114
Horns effect, 52–53
Human resources department
consulting about discharge, 81
grievance referral to the director of, 30
sexual harassment reports to, 120
suspension notification to, 76
as a termination interview site, 85

Implied legally enforceable contracts, verbal and written evidence of, 72–73
Inappropriate behaviors, identification of, 26–28
Incidence of substance abuse, 91
Incident record, example, 45
Information, communicating to employees, 2
Infractions, levels and procedures for managing, 23–25
Intent of disciplinary action, 1
Interview
disciplinary, 62–64
performance appraisal, 54–55
termination, 84–89
Interviewer's Evaluation Form, 128–130
Involuntary termination. *See* Discharge

Job design, and compliance with performance standards, 121

Job security, employee handbook entry on, 73
Jury service
and discharge decisions, 82
exception to employment-at-will, 72
Just cause termination, 73
and progressive discipline, 9

Labor Statistics, Bureau of, reported incidence of substance abuse, 91
Language
confirming suitability of, 28
positive, 56
Last chance agreement for substance abuse, 99
Lateness, 103
Legal action
documentation for use in, 65
for negligent hiring practices, 124
Legal requirements
a discipline process for meeting, 11
review of substance abuse policy to assure meeting, 99
Legislation
Age Discrimination in Employment Act of 1967, 82
Americans with Disabilities Act of 1990, 82
Civil Rights Act of 1964, 72, 81, 119
Consolidated Omnibus Budget Reconciliation Act (COBRA) of 19, 76, 78
Drug Free Workplace Act of 1988, 92
Employee Retirement Income Security Act of 1974, 82
Employee Retirement Income Security Act (ERISA) of 1974, 78
Occupational Safety and Health Act of 1970, 82

Pregnancy Discrimination Act of 1978, 82
Retirement Equity Act (REA) of 1984, 78
Tax Reform Act (TRA) of 1986, 78
Vietnam-Era Veterans' Readjustment Assistance Act of 1974, 82
Length of service, and rating of employee performance, 53
Leniency error, 52
Letters of reference, caution in wording, 78
Listening
during a disciplinary interview, 63–64
during a termination interview, 85, 88
Listening skills, 35–37
for coaching, 35–36, 38
Logbook
supervisor's, 65
supervisor's, example, 44
supervisor's, example of verbal warning documentation, 66
Lost-time accidents, 108

Manager, review of documented interviews, 65
Managerial employees, 19
Match, between an employee and the job, 122
Medications, over-the counter or prescribed, that affect job performance, 97
Motivation
for good attendance, 108
and performance, 122
Mutual respect, emphasis on, supervisors' training, 135–136
Mutual understanding, reaching in a disciplinary interview, 64

National Drug Control Strategy, 92
National Guard service
and discharge decisions, 82

exception to employment-at-will, 72
National Institute on Drug Abuse, reported incidence of substance abuse, 91
No-fault attendance policy, 107
Nonverbal language, reading during appraisal interviews, 55
See also Body language
Notice
  to a marginal employee, example, 58
  termination, 75

Objectives
  of attendance policies, 107
  of employee assistance programs, 100
  of training in effective communication, 137, 138, 139, 140
Occupational Safety and Health Act of 1970, and discharge decisions, 82
Open-door policy for resolving grievances, 28–29
Orientation, safety training during, 110

Past performance, and conduct rule violations, 62
Pay for unwarranted suspension, 75
Peer review for resolving grievances, 29, 30
Pensions of terminated employees, 78
Performance, 35–59
  improvement through discipline, 1–2
Performance appraisal, 2–4, 13, 35, 43–59
  of a marginal employee, 56–59
  versus performance management, 37
Performance management, 35
  cycle of, 36
  versus performance appraisal, 37

Performance standards, 2
  clear identification of, 11
  communication during orientation and training, 33
  development of, 13, 14
  example, head cook, 15–19
Personal communication goals, 149
Personal references, 126
Personnel policies and procedures, discipline example, 22–25
Place for a termination interview, 85
Plan of action for improving performance, 59
Policy review and revision, employee feedback in, 135
Policy statement
  example, 22
  on severance pay, 76
  pay, example, 77
Positive behavior, reinforcement of, 135
Positive discipline, 5–6
Positive feedback to reward employees for good attendance, 107–108
Positive reinforcement
  and corrective action, 70
  emphasis on, supervisors' training, 135–136
  of improvement, 5–6
Praise
  as informal coaching, 40
  letter of thanks, example, 41
  to motivate good attendance, 108
  recognition memo, example, 42
Preemployment testing, 123–124
Pregnancy Discrimination Act of 1978, and discharge decisions, 82
Preparation for a performance appraisal, 55
Probationary period, 28
Problem, treating unwanted behavior as a, 5
Problem areas, open discussion of during appraisal reviews, 56

Problem resolution procedure. *See* Grievance procedure
Problem-solving sessions for supervisors, 135
Process of discipline
flowchart, 3
steps in, 2
Professional reputation damages, awards in wrongful discharge judgments, 71
Progressive discipline, 6–10
and substance abuse, 97
Public policy, and exceptions to employment-at-will, 72
Public records as a resource in reference checking, 124, 125
Punishment in the traditional approach to discipline, 4–5
Punitive damages, awards in wrongful discharge judgments, 71

Quiz
communications training workshop, 150
safety training, 115–116

Rating categories, 47, 52
Rating errors, 52–54
REA. *See* Retirement Equity Act
Reasonable standards, reviewing before discipline is instituted, 27
Recency error, 53
Recommendations of peer review committees, 30
Reference checks, 123–124
References, letters of, 78
Referrals to employee assistance programs, 100
Refusal to perform illegal acts
and discharge decisions, 82
exception to employment-at-will, 72
Rehabilitation options in substance abuse, 98–99

Reinforcement of positive behavior, 135
Responsibility, employee's, 4, 6, 135
and employee assistance plans, 100–101
establishing in a counseling session, 9
in the positive approach to discipline, 5
for solutions to problem behavior, 64
Retaliation for whistle-blowing
and discharge decisions, 82
exception to employment-at-will, 72
Retirement Equity Act (REA) of 1984, 78
Rights of employees to appeal a disciplinary decision, 12
Role model, supervisor, owner, or manager as, 114
Role-playing in supervisors' training, 135, 144

Safety committees, 114
Safety hazards, 108, 110–116
training quiz, 115–116
Safety training, 110, 114
Salary review, separating from performance appraisal, 54
Selection procedures, 123–134
communication of performance standards during hiring, 2
Self-esteem, maintaining an employee's, 70, 88
Self-evaluation, 54, 55
of attendance-related behaviors, 118
Self-respect
maintaining an employee's, 37, 70
and the traditional approach to discipline, 4
Separation form, 80
Seriousness of conduct rule violations, 62
Severance pay, 76

Sexual harassment, 119–120
Significance of behavior,
    communicating to
    employees, 68
Solution to a problem with conduct
    rules, 9
Step procedure for resolving
    grievances, 29
Strategies for reducing employee
    defensiveness, 38
Subjective evaluations, error of, 52
Substance abuse, 91–103
  defined, 98
  policy on, 93–99
    example, 94–97
Supervisors, training of, 134–135
  for managing substance abuse
      problems, 101–103
Suspension, 70
  alternative to on-the-spot
      firing, 75

Tax Reform Act (TRA) of 1986, 78
Termination, 71–89
  after failure to meet performance
      standards, 57
  policy for, 75–78
  reducing the need for, 6
Termination interview, 84–89
  final paycheck presented
      during, 76
Time limits in a grievance
    process, 30
Timing of a termination
    interview, 85
Tools, and compliance with
    performance standards, 121
TRA. *See* Tax Reform Act
Traditional approach to discipline,
    4–5
  progressive discipline in, 6–9
Training (magazine), 43
Transfer, 78, 81

Union participation
  and discharge decisions, 82
  exception to employment-at-will,
      72
Unions
  and employee responsibility, 6
  grievance procedures of, 28
  representation during substance
      abuse searches, 96

Vacation time, payment on
    termination, 78
Verbal warning
  documentation of, 67
  in the traditional system, 7–9
Vested pensions, 78
Vietnam-Era Veterans'
    Readjustment Assistance Act
    of 1974, and discharge
    decisions, 82
Voluntary termination (quitting), 71

Warning notice, example, 69
Willful misconduct, evaluating, 62
Workers' compensation records for
    reference checking, 124, 126
Working conditions, safety of, 110
Work performance, evaluation and
    coaching to improve, 38–39
Work record, and conduct rule
    violations, 62
Written complaint in a grievance
    procedure, 29–30
Written discipline notice, signing
    of, 64
Written procedures, substance
    abuse policy, 93–97
Wrongful discharge
  avoiding, 57
  suits for, 71